TO MY HUSBAND, ANDREW, FOR BEING
MY BIGGEST SUPPORTER, ALWAYS.

THE BETTER HABITS WORKBOOK

THE BETTER HABITS WORKBOOK

Exercises for Getting Unstuck, Changing Your Behavior, and Reaching Your Goals

Stephanie Sorady Arias, MSW

R
ROCKRIDGE
PRESS

First Rockridge Press trade paperback edition 2022

Rockridge Press and the Rockridge Press logo are trademarks or registered trademarks of Callisto Media Inc. and/or its affiliates in the United States and other countries and may not be used without written permission.

For general information on our other products and services, please contact our Customer Care Department within the United States at (866) 744-2665, or outside the United States at (510) 253-0500.

Paperback ISBN: 978-1-68539-284-0 | eBook ISBN: 978-1-68539-501-8

Manufactured in the United States of America

Interior and Cover Designer: Tess Evans
Art Producer: Sue Bischofberger
Editor: Eun H. Jeong
Production Editor: Jax Berman
Production Manager: Martin Worthington

10 9 8 7 6 5 4 3 2 1 0

CONTENTS

INTRODUCTION

Welcome to *The Better Habits Workbook*. This workbook will provide you with the opportunity to get unstuck, build positive habits, and reach your goals. In this workbook, you will find fun, effective tools to guide you each step of the way. My name is Stephanie Sorady, and I'm an associate clinical social worker based in Los Angeles, California. I have been working in the field of mental health for five years and have experience supporting the healthy habits of folks from a variety of backgrounds and experiences. I first became interested in habit building and behavior modification through my own desire to live a happier and healthier life. I often felt frustrated and wondered if I simply did not have the "willpower" to avoid my bad habits and stay consistent with more positive ones. But in my research, I found that successful habit change is not about willpower–it's about having the right information, strategies, and structures in place. I have since used these strategies to support and accomplish some of my smallest and largest goals and have had the privilege of guiding my therapy clients to do the same. I am so excited to share what I've learned with you here.

In my work as a mental health clinician, I am constantly amazed by how capable of positive change people truly are if they are given the right tools. I incorporate Cognitive Behavioral Therapy (CBT), Behavior Modification, and mindfulness techniques into the work I do with my clients. You will learn and utilize these same evidence-based skills throughout this workbook. One of the many elements I love about my work is witnessing how seemingly small changes make a major impact on people's lives. Every aspect of this workbook has been curated to support you in making your own small but powerful changes. In these pages, you will find valuable information along with affirmations, prompts, practices, and exercises to help you put this new knowledge into practice. You will learn how to create healthy habits, how to let go of unhealthy habits, and how to successfully set and achieve goals.

Please note that even though a workbook is a great way to work through a habit-change journey and process a range of complicated feelings, any ongoing or debilitating feelings of depression, anxiety, or other mental health concerns should be addressed by a medical professional. This book is not a replacement for a therapist, medication, or medical treatment. As a psychotherapist who has also been in therapy, I truly mean it when I say there is no shame in seeking help or treatment. On page 162, you will find additional resources for finding professional help.

Although embarking on the journey to change your habits may feel intimidating at first, please remember you can go at your own pace. I am here to guide you through this process, but you are in total control of what your journey looks like. You are more than welcome to take breaks as needed to process this information.

The goal of this workbook is to learn and use evidence-based habit strategies that support your lifestyle, values, and goals. Be patient and compassionate with yourself as you embark on making these changes. The more patient and compassionate you are, the more likely it is that these habit changes will be sustainable in the long term. Lastly, it's important you believe, as I do, that you are capable of getting unstuck, changing your habits, and achieving your goals. You can do this!

HOW TO USE THIS BOOK

This workbook is divided into two parts. The first part provides foundational material to help you understand habits, behaviors, and the evidence-based techniques to build good habits that are referred to throughout the remainder of the book. The second part will guide you through identifying your goals and initiating and sustaining positive habit change through the use of several tools. Affirmations will help you stay positive and overcome challenging thoughts; prompts will provide you an opportunity for reflection; practices will give you the chance to engage in activities outside of the book; and in-book exercises will help you implement your positive changes.

This workbook was designed to be worked on sequentially, to offer structured, specific guidance on how to identify and define good and bad habits, and how to break free from the bad habits to make space for the good ones. I encourage you to work your way through each chapter at your own pace. You may notice you enjoy doing one chapter per week, or that you specifically like using this workbook first thing in the morning; do whatever works best for you. Remember, you are meant to use this as a resource to support your unique needs. After you've gone through this workbook from start to finish, you can always flip back to specific exercises depending on what you need. Lastly, I highly suggest you stay curious and engaged when working through this book to help you learn and utilize the skills you need to support your goals. You can always keep what works best for you and set the rest aside.

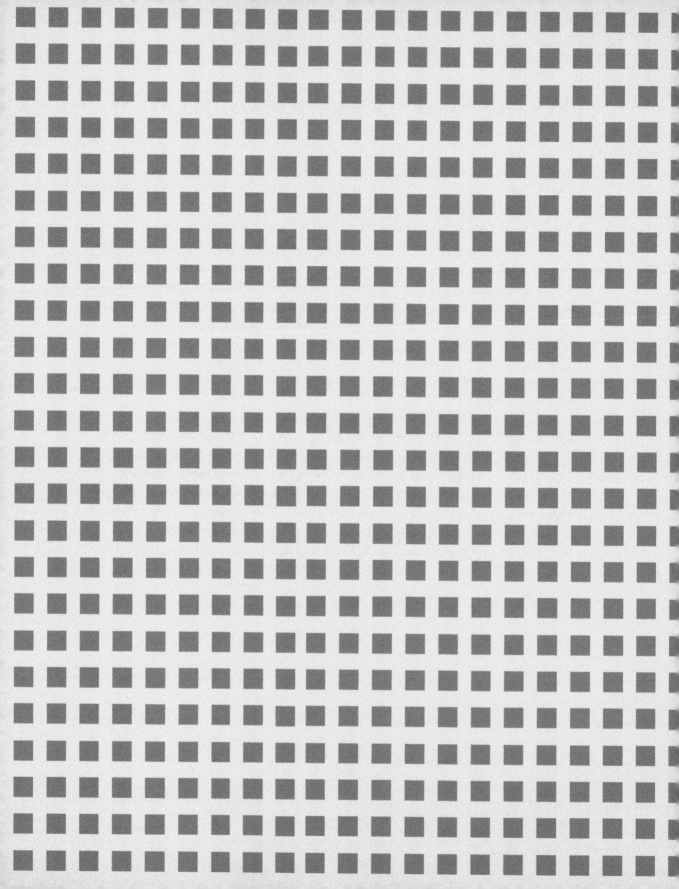

UNDERSTANDING HABITS

Whether you recognize it or not, your daily life is already made up of dozens of habits. From brushing your teeth in the morning to the last thing you do before going to bed, habits are currently shaping your goals, health, and success. Developing clarity and self-awareness around your behaviors is the first step on the path to lasting habit change.

This workbook will empower you to be more intentional about your habits and ultimately create a fulfilling life. To get started, part I of this workbook will provide clarity on what habits are, what makes a habit good or bad, and what proven strategies can help you break free from limiting habits and, at the same time, create healthy new ones.

Demystifying Habits

This chapter will cover the basics and provide answers to common questions about habits, such as: What is a habit? Where do habits come from? What makes a habit good or bad? How can cycles of self-sabotage be overcome? Concepts you can expect to see in chapter 1 include misunderstandings about willpower and the importance of aligning with your values.

Each idea explored in this chapter is foundational to the rest of this workbook, as well as to your success during the process of changing your habits and working toward your goals. Remember that a lot of the following material may be new to you, so be compassionate with yourself as you take time to learn and grow. Conversely, if you're already familiar with a concept or strategy, it's recommended that you approach that information with a fresh perspective. Remaining curious and engaged will support you and your goals.

Tanya Tackles an Unhealthy Habit

Tanya works as an administrator in an office and is great at her job. However, when more clients started coming in and there was no additional staff to help out, Tanya's stress levels increased. To manage this stress, Tanya started snacking on potato chips during her breaks. Every day at the same time she would go to the vending machine. After a couple of weeks, Tanya noticed she was feeling sluggish after her breaks instead of recharged. It became hard for her to focus and stay alert. Even after new staff was hired to help and her workload was back to normal, Tanya kept buying her chips like clockwork.

Tanya's coworker, Mateo, noticed that she was distracted each afternoon and asked if she was okay. Tanya shared that her change in focus and energy began when she started eating chips every afternoon to reduce stress at work. However, her chip habit was not reducing stress; in fact, it was having negative impacts on her health. Tanya shared that she wanted to stop, but could not break the habit. Every day she would walk down the hall to the vending machine and buy her chips. Tanya was beginning to feel bad about herself, believing she had no "self-control." Mateo asked Tanya how she was managing her stress outside of eating chips, and much to Tanya's own surprise, she did not have an answer. Fortunately, Mateo had an idea. He said he wanted to walk more for his own health, and he suggested that they go on walks together during break to help with her stress. Tanya happily agreed. She asked if they could walk in the opposite direction of the vending machine to limit temptations.

Soon, Tanya was able to quit her chip habit and replace it with walking. Tanya now comes back from her breaks less stressed and more energized. The experience helped her see that she didn't need more "self-control." She now recognized that she simply needed more self-awareness about how different habits impact her health, along with a clear strategy to manage stress in a positive way.

What Is a Habit, Really?

Every day you make thousands of decisions. It would be exhausting for any one person to sit and ponder each of those decisions as the need for them occurred. It's important for your mental and emotional health that some decisions become automatic over time. Automating certain decisions conserves your mental and emotional energy for when you need it most. That is one of the many ways that habits can help!

Habits are behavior patterns you do regularly, and in many cases without thinking. For example, you may have the habit of immediately getting out of bed every morning when your alarm rings. Or you may have the habit of hitting snooze every morning the moment your alarm goes off. In both instances, the habits are repeated and automatic. One quality that distinguishes a habit from a behavior is that behaviors are often reactive, but habits are automated consequences of decisions you've made again and again. Another distinction between habits and behaviors is that a behavior can be done once, but a habit is repeated either consciously or unconsciously.

Your daily life is filled with habits you've created both with and without realizing it. From washing your hands to meditating, your habits can take many forms. You may perceive some of your habits as good and others as bad depending on the results they provide (this will be explored more later in this chapter). Habits shape your health, relationships, self-esteem, and overall wellness. No matter how small habits may seem, they are the building blocks of your life. It is these seemingly small habits that shape who you are. Keep the above definition in mind as you continue throughout this workbook. Now that you've established what defines a habit, it's time to take a closer look at how they are formed.

Where Do Habits Come From?

Habits are created both consciously and unconsciously. That means that some habits are formed intentionally, but others are created without your full awareness. For example, biting your nails is often an unconscious habit, whereas sticking to your workout routine is a much more conscious one. You may have noticed that sometimes you pick up habits with ease but struggle to adopt others. If you've struggled with habit change goals in the past, please know that you are not alone. It can be a challenge to identify where your habits come from. Understanding your behavior helps to clarify this mystery.

You may be wondering, *"If some habits are conscious and others are unconscious, then how are habits formed?"* Research shows that habits are created as the result of a "behavior chain" or "behavior loop" that is repeated over time. A behavior chain looks like this: antecedent ➔ behavior ➔ consequence. For example, you pass by a restaurant and smell French fries. The cue is smelling French fries, which prompts the thought, "I'm hungry." This is followed by the action of going inside the restaurant to buy the fries. Finally, the immediate consequence is that you feel satisfied by the fries you ate.

As the example illustrates, antecedents typically kick off the behavior loop and come in many forms like emotions, environments, smells, or even certain people. Following an antecedent, your thought in response to a cue will vary depending on many factors. Your actions–the potential habit–may be perceived as good or bad depending on short- and long-term consequences. For some habits it only takes a few repetitions of the behavior loop for the habit to be ingrained. It may take longer for other habits to become automatic. But generally, it is known that the more a behavior loop repeats, the more a habit becomes ingrained in your life. The habits that you currently have in your life are the results of this type of behavior pattern.

What Makes a Habit Good or Bad?

It's important to note that few habits can be objectively classified as good or bad. What makes a habit good or bad depends on two simple factors: the consequences of that habit, and how you evaluate those consequences. Therefore, you will be evaluating which habits are good and which are bad in the context of your life.

A bad habit will have negative consequences on your health and well-being, while a good habit will have positive consequences. However, it's important to note that bad habits may feel good for a little while. For example, say you have the habit of gossiping. Gossiping may feel good in the moment, but it could negatively impact your relationships in the long-term. If you evaluate this habit, you can see how you may consider it a bad habit.

In order to decide which habits you would like to build and which ones you'd like to remove from your life, it's important that you learn how to evaluate your current habits. Throughout this workbook, there will be many opportunities for you to gain clarity on your habits. For now, start by bringing awareness to your habits and the consequences. When starting a habit, you can ask yourself, "What are the consequences I want to see?" to clarify if this habit is a good or bad fit for your goals.

Other questions to help you evaluate a habit include:

- How does this habit make me feel?

- How do I want to feel?

- How does this habit impact me in the short term?

- How does this habit impact me in the long term?

- What are my short- and long-term goals?

- Does this habit help me reach those goals?

Answering these questions will empower you to be the judge of what makes a habit good or bad. You can also revisit these questions throughout your habit-change process whenever you need additional clarity and/or guidance.

How to Overcome Urges, Temptations, and Self-Sabotage

If some of your habits have negative consequences, then why do you keep doing them? You likely repeat habits because the immediate consequence, or reward, satisfies you somehow. What qualifies as an immediate reward varies greatly from person to person. For example, sometimes a bad habit can relieve stress in the moment but cause more stress over time. Therefore, even if you know a habit is bad for you in the long run (i.e., smoking cigarettes), you may continue to engage in that habit because of urges, desires, temptations, or self-sabotaging behavior. Remember, it's not uncommon for folks to engage in bad habits, and it's absolutely possible to eliminate and replace them with good habits.

Even with these negative factors at play, behavioral changes can still be made. You don't keep bad habits because you lack intelligence or willpower; you just don't have the right strategies in place—yet! If you want to start a new healthy habit or quit an old, unhealthy one, but temptations keep getting in the way, go back to the behavior loop. By changing parts of the loop, you can change your habits. This workbook will help you do just that.

IT'S NOT ABOUT WILLPOWER

There's a common myth that all it takes to create or quit a habit is willpower, and many people often cite their lack of it as being responsible for their struggle with changing habits. The myth of willpower can lead to feelings of discouragement or even shame. Some folks feel so utterly without it that they might not even try to change, thinking to themselves, "What's the point?" But in reality, it's not that simple. Sheer force of will, self-control, or self-discipline don't often make or break habits.

Habits are formed, built, and sustained by many different factors. It is the small and consistent decisions made throughout daily life that form habits. It's also important to note that habits are regularly formed, and because of this, it's normal that you may struggle to make or break habits in your life. You can always start again with the next decision you make. When thinking about how you would like to change your habits, remember that you have endless opportunities to try again and make new choices. So, there is no shame; only compassion, understanding, and continuous growth on your journey to build the life that you want for yourself.

Forming and changing habits is about self-awareness and creating strategies and support systems that work for you, rather than reliance on some kind of internal discipline. Self-awareness and thoughtful strategies, not willpower, will help you overcome temptation. With the right knowledge and tools, you are capable of changing your habits and achieving your goals.

Later in this book, you will learn about evidence-based approaches like Cognitive Behavioral Therapy (CBT) and Behavior Modification and how they can help you understand and shape your thoughts and behaviors to form positive changes in your life. Think of them as tools for your toolbox that will make habit change easier and long-lasting. Give each technique an honest try to understand what works best for you. Some tools may resonate with you more than others and that's okay. Experimenting with different techniques is a part of the self-awareness process that will support you on this journey. These evidence-based techniques will help you rely less and less on willpower.

This process can be hard, especially at the beginning, because you are going against your automatic urges. Don't be concerned if some habits change more slowly than others. As you learn and practice key strategies for habit change, it's important that you are compassionate with yourself. This often means reminding yourself that it's okay to make mistakes or have setbacks. Approach habit change with compassion, and you will be able to stick with your efforts through the ups and downs to ultimately create lasting changes.

How Will Changing Your Habits Change You?

Habits are the building blocks of life. They are the seemingly small, but significant, actions you take regularly that impact every area of your physical, mental, and social well-being. Habit change requires effort and there can be obstacles along the journey. Given that you picked up this book, not only do you recognize that habits form who you are, but also that changing your habits can ultimately change your life. This insight shows that you're already on your way to receiving the benefits of habit change!

Recognizing the value of changing your habits will help you remain motivated and inspired. Changing your habits can change your life for the better. There are numerous benefits to changing your habits and some of the most significant ones will be covered within this workbook. Making changes to your habits can allow you to align with your values, improve your health, boost happiness, and strengthen your personality.

You may be wondering, how can habits impact so much? Simply put, habits provide you with the structure to show up as the best version of yourself. Habits are the constants in your life, and they build the foundation of who you are on a day-to-day basis. Imagine the version of yourself you've always wanted to be. Visualize who they are and what habits make up their lifestyle. This is your encouraging reminder that you are already capable of becoming that person. Your habits will be the key steps guiding you to live out that vision.

Align Actions with Values

Habits directly impact your ability to live in alignment with your values. Habits are a way of embodying and committing to your values. For example, if you are someone who values punctuality, but you engage in habits that always make you late, then you are not currently aligned with that value. Releasing the unhealthy habits you've acquired will align you with the value of health. You can also create new habits to do the same. For instance, if you value compassion, you can build a habit of performing one compassionate act every day. Think of your habits as your values in action.

Improve Your Health and Well-Being

Unsurprisingly, habits have a large impact on your health and well-being. You can use the techniques in this workbook to improve your physical, mental, and emotional health. There is a strong connection between your body and your mind. If you're healthier, you will tend to be happier too! Start by identifying areas of your health and well-being that you would like to improve. Would you like to improve your physical health? Increase your energy throughout the day? Reduce your stress? You get to decide what aspects of your health and wellness mean the most to you as you embark on this habit-change journey.

Some ideas for habits that tend to improve health and wellness include exercising, stretching, drinking water, meditating, maintaining healthy relationships, practicing gratitude, and other self-care activities that you would enjoy. You can glean inspiration for habits that tend to improve health from the various examples in this book, or create your own. The key to improving your health through habits is identifying what works for you.

Strengthen Your Personality

Do you want to harness your unique strengths and live to your fullest potential? Possessing the correct habits, and the right strategies behind them, can get you there. Habits allow you to automate tasks, reduce decision fatigue, and maximize your unique strengths. When things like exercise, taking vitamins, journaling, and staying hydrated become habits rather than something you struggle with every day to do, then there's more energy to be creative and solve problems.

You can create habits that play into your strengths. For example, if you are a naturally social person and you want to become a better friend, you can create a habit of reaching out to a friend once per week to check in and see if they need anything. Or you can work on building habits you may have struggled with in the past, but that you feel are key to your personality. For example, if you currently have the habit of arriving to social functions late, but you identify as someone who is considerate and punctual, you can work on building the habit of being on time to strengthen this aspect of yourself. When deciding what habits you'd like to build and release, you can ask yourself, "What habits would reflect the best parts of my personality?"

How to Figure Out What Habits to Change

As you learn various strategies for habit change, you will also want to figure out what habits you want to change and/or build. The first step in doing this is to get clear on the goals you would like to achieve. After you've identified your goals, you can get clear on the habits that would be helpful to change. You can ask yourself, *"What habits could I develop to support these goals? What habits do I currently have that are barriers to achieving these goals?"*

To get a head start on this part of the process, begin by "brain-dumping" ideas you have for goals you might want to set. A brain-dump is a simple tool to get your creative juices flowing. During a brain-dump, you write down every single idea that comes to mind. It's important that you do not censor yourself or judge any of the ideas. Your only objective of a brain-dump is to get the potential ideas for habit change out of your head and onto a page for you to review. After you've "dumped" all of the ideas out onto a page, the next step is to group the ideas into different areas of your life. These areas may include relationships, work, health, spirituality, and self-care. These categories are not fixed or mandatory. You can create whatever life sectors make sense for you.

Feel free to keep the list of potential habits handy to reference as you continue through this workbook. Completing these two steps, and referring back to your brain-dump, will set you up for success in the chapters to come. Remember that it is okay to alter, remove, or add goals as you gain additional clarity.

Key Takeaways

■ Habits are behavior patterns you do regularly and, in many cases, without thinking.

■ Habits are created as the result of a "behavior chain" that consists of antecedents, behaviors, and consequences.

■ Whether or not a habit is good or bad depends on your perception of the consequences of that habit.

■ It's not a matter of willpower. The right habit strategies can help you overcome temptations.

■ Changing your habits will help you improve your health, align you with your values, and strengthen your personality.

Now that you are equipped with knowledge about habits, you will explore different strategies for changing habits in the next chapter. Continue to stay engaged and you will see amazing results!

CHAPTER 2

Proven Techniques for Changing Habits

This chapter will take a closer look at evidence-based techniques and modalities for changing habits, and at the principles behind habit change that have been introduced so far. Although there are a wide range of approaches that can be used for modifying habits, those covered here will be Cognitive Behavioral Therapy (CBT), Behavior Modification, and mindfulness. Each of these approaches has its differences and similarities. You'll discover that behind each of these approaches to changing habits lies the principle of breaking big problems into small steps in order to set realistic goals and build a program of small, but consistent, change. This core principle allows you to create gradual and sustainable change over time.

CBT, Behavior Modification, and mindfulness are the tools that will comprise your toolbox for meaningful habit change. Remember, each of the following techniques can be altered to fit your needs. Take note of what works best for you, and use those methods consistently to see positive change. With these tools, you are capable of making whatever changes you desire.

Jamal Develops Mindful Habits

Jamal wondered why he never had enough time. He felt extremely busy but had little to show for it at the end of the day. As a result, Jamal felt frustrated and drained, and he couldn't spend time doing things he enjoyed. When he brought this up with his therapist, she asked Jamal to walk her through how he spent his time. Jamal struggled to recount his schedule and activities, sharing, "I think I'm on autopilot." Jamal realized he was not being intentional about his time.

Jamal's therapist recommended he practice mindfulness habits. Mindfulness may help him be more aware of how he was spending his time and the impact on his thoughts and feelings. With more self-awareness, he would also be able to use mindfulness to help him go about his day more intentionally and efficiently. Some mindfulness habits that she suggested included regular check-ins with his body and thoughts and using deep breathing to find focus and calm.

As he implemented mindfulness habits into his life, Jamal developed a new awareness of how he was spending his time. He was doing many tasks at once, and as such, he would often lose focus, skip steps, and ultimately have to redo things. He also became more aware of how his habits were negatively impacting his time and feelings.

With this new self-awareness and mindfulness techniques to help him find calm and focus, Jamal began implementing new habits one by one, being intentional with his time and behavior, and working through setbacks with patience and without judgment. Even though it wasn't easy, and it took practice and time, Jamal's mindful habits gave him back his time and energy. He no longer felt like he didn't have enough time in his life and was able to enjoy more of the things he loved.

CBT for Habit Change

Cognitive Behavioral Therapy (CBT) is a psychological school of thought and treatment technique used to improve mental health and well-being. Some disorders that can benefit from CBT include depression, anxiety, panic, phobias, and addictions. CBT was founded in the 1960s by psychiatrist Aaron Beck who recognized how certain thoughts contributed to emotional disturbances. According to 2021 research conducted by the Beck Institute, more than 2,000 studies have demonstrated the effectiveness of CBT for changing thoughts, emotions, and behaviors. CBT has been a staple in the field of habit change for many years and continues to evolve and improve.

CBT is a practical approach to changing the "wiring" in your brain to both undo and create habits. "Wiring" basically refers to the immediate actions and reactions you may experience. CBT is one of the most widely researched psychological approaches. A 2012 independent analysis, conducted by Hofmann et al, looked at 269 CBT studies and reported enormous behavior change overall, especially related to anxiety, anger, and general stress for individuals, couples, and groups of various ages and backgrounds. This study revealed how CBT techniques empower people to change their thoughts, feelings, and behaviors to live happier and healthier lives.

One of the basic concepts of CBT is the cognitive triangle. The cognitive triangle is an illustration that shows how thoughts, emotions, and behaviors are all connected. Each part of the triangle is important and influences the others. The more you understand the cognitive triangle, the easier it will be to leverage it for positive habit change.

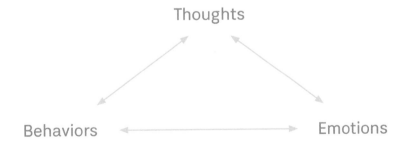

How Thoughts Influence Your Emotions and Behaviors

Thoughts are your interpretation of a situation. A simple example is: On a rainy day one person may see the rain and think, "It's a beautiful day," but another person thinks, "What a terrible day." This example illustrates how thoughts are not always objective or factual. Automatic thoughts are instant, habitual, and often unconscious. But regardless of how objective or factual a thought may be, thoughts have a direct impact on a person's feelings and actions. For example, imagine you greet a neighbor on the street, but they do not respond. Your automatic thought might be, "They don't like me." That thought makes you angry. The feeling of anger may influence how you greet your neighbor in the future. A simple automatic thought can have tangible and lasting consequences.

How Emotions Influence Your Thoughts and Behaviors

Emotions are feelings, such as happiness, sadness, worry, and anger. Just as thoughts can influence emotions, emotions can influence thoughts. If someone is feeling positive, they are more likely to have positive thoughts. Emotions can also impact your behaviors. Referring to the example above, it may be possible to see how the thought, "They don't like me," led you to feel angry. The emotion of anger may lead you to behave rudely toward that neighbor the next time you see them. But what if the emotion was different? For example, if instead of feeling anger at the thought, "They don't like me," you felt neutral, you may behave indifferently the next time you see them.

How Behaviors Influence Your Thoughts and Emotions

Behaviors are actions (or a lack of action) in response to a situation. Behaviors are the habits you are looking to change. Behaviors are influenced by, and in turn influence, your thoughts and emotions. So far, you've seen examples of how thoughts and emotions can impact behavior; now consider an example of the reverse. If you want to feel more confident when you walk into a room, you can choose to behave confidently by standing up straight. Walking in with straight posture can make you feel more confident. Behaving more confidently can lead to actually feeling more confident and thinking confident thoughts, such as "I am capable."

So, you see that each element in the cognitive triangle can strongly influence the other elements. Overall, it's evident that your thoughts, emotions, and behaviors play an impactful role in your life.

The ABCs of Behavior Modification

Another modality that has been shown to help habit change is Behavior Modification. Behavior Modification aims to either increase or decrease certain behaviors (such as habits). Behavior Modification has similarities to CBT in that both of these approaches can create positive habit change by analyzing factors that can create habits. There are, however, key differences between these two approaches.

Although CBT focuses primarily on thought patterns, Behavior Modification focuses on the behavior loop previously discussed in chapter 1. In this approach, you want to make changes in the loop of antecedent, behavior, and consequence. There is notable evidence from 2021 research conducted by Scott, Jain, and Cogburn, that supports the use of behavioral techniques to reduce unwanted habits or teach and reinforce positive habits. In my own work, I've supported clients in implementing Behavior Modification to successfully improve their health, reduce stress, and strengthen communication skills. The key to making these changes is to be as self-aware and objective as possible. Now is a good time to take a closer look at antecedents, behaviors, and consequences.

Antecedent

An antecedent, or cue, is anything that triggers a behavior, whether desired or undesired. An antecedent can also be referred to as a "cue" or "prompt." It can be a specific place, time of day, person, or another behavior that happens immediately before. An antecedent can be strategically implemented to illicit a desired behavior. For instance, if you want to journal every day, you would consider if there's a specific time of day, place, or other behavior that could be your antecedent on a regular basis. Maybe you drink a cup of tea every morning without fail, so you use that behavior as the cue to start journaling. With repetition of the antecedent and behavior sequence, you can develop the habit of journaling every day.

Behavior

The behavior is the action, or habit, that you are either trying to foster or replace. The antecedent prompts the behavior. Referring to the previous example, your antecedent is the cup of tea you have each morning, and your behavior is journaling after your cup of tea. Finishing the cup of tea cues the behavior of a journaling practice. The behavior is also influenced by how you feel after doing it. After you're done journaling, you may feel more mental and emotional clarity as a result. That consequence will reinforce the behavior. Remember, behaviors are either good or bad depending on the consequences. Throughout this process, you decide which behaviors you'd like to release or implement.

Consequence

Consequences are the outcomes of behaviors. Like behaviors, consequences can be perceived as good or bad. Perception depends on your goals. Consequences can be reframed as celebrations to help reinforce good behavior. In the example, journaling has the positive consequence of providing increased mental and emotional clarity. You can further reinforce this behavior by adding a celebration to the consequence. An example of a celebration might be taking your cup of tea and journal to your favorite outdoor place once a week. A common challenge with consequences is that many behaviors create immediate rewards but carry long-term negative consequences. All behaviors have consequences. It is important to raise awareness of consequences, both short-term and long-term, in order to eliminate unwanted habits and build better ones.

Mindfulness for Habit Change

Another effective strategy for habit change is mindfulness. The difference between mindfulness practices and the other techniques covered is that mindfulness is a way of being in your daily life instead of an isolated practice for breaking down behavior. Mindfulness is the ability to be fully aware in the moment. It encompasses many practices and has been a part of many cultures, particularly Eastern traditions, for thousands of years. Research has caught up with ancient wisdom as many studies show mindfulness can help with improving mood, boosting positive emotions, increasing self-awareness, and deepening self. Another benefit is that mindfulness can be used to enhance both CBT and Behavior Modification techniques.

For example, mindfulness can help you identify the changes you'd like to make. Being more mindful of feelings in your body, mind, and spirit can give you clarity on whether a habit is good or bad. Ask yourself, "What reactions do I notice in response to a specific habit? Do the consequences of a habit hinder or support my goals?" These questions can help to inform whether you'd like to release, keep, or strengthen a habit.

Mindfulness tools can also be used to replace a bad habit in your habit loop. If you're engaging in a bad habit because you are overwhelmed, stressed, bored, or avoiding a painful emotion, consider substituting the bad habit for a moment of mindfulness. For example, if you mindlessly scroll on your phone (behavior) every time you're stressed (emotion/antecedent), you can swap out scrolling on your phone for five minutes of mindful, deep breathing. Overall, mindfulness can support your habit changes and general well-being, either on its own or in conjunction with CBT and Behavior Modification.

Breaking Big Problems into Small Habits

If you set big goals, you may be likely to encounter big problems. For example, if you set the goal to run a marathon, you may encounter a variety of big problems related to motivation, physical fitness, training schedules, and other logistical details. Encountering big problems is normal and can be managed through the tools and strategies covered in this workbook. Each technique helps you break down big problems into small but meaningful habits. Small habits are easier to change and remain consistent over time, often because they feel less overwhelming and are simpler to engage in. Once you've mastered a small habit change, you can build upon it to create even larger changes.

Going back to the marathon example, you can first start with developing the habit of running one block every day. As you develop this habit, you can create small milestones, such as adding another block every week. One additional block may not seem like a lot in the moment, but as your running habit continues to build and grow, you will reach the distance and physical endurance needed for running a full marathon.

Think back to the case study at the start of this chapter. When Jamal felt like he didn't have enough time, the first habit he developed was raising his awareness of the present moment. Although this habit may seem small, it was in fact the foundation for his very impactful lifestyle changes. Don't forget that you can do the same!

BAD HABITS VS. ADDICTIONS

At this point, you may be wondering, "What is the difference between a bad habit and an addiction?" There are key differences between the two. According to the American Society of Addiction Medicine, addiction is a treatable medical condition that is the result of complicated factors, like brain chemistry, genetics, environment, and a person's life experiences. Per their definition, a person with an addiction will compulsively continue to use substances or engage in behaviors despite negative consequences. Note that addiction isn't limited to using a certain substance, but can be any compulsive behavior that is harmful to the person engaging in that behavior and those around them.

There are a few key differences between a bad habit and an addiction. One of the main differences is the word *compulsive*, meaning a person has less control over the behavior. With an addiction, many people report feeling "powerless" when it comes to the substance or behavior. Secondly, addictions will severely impact multiple areas of a person's life, like health, relationships, career, self-esteem, and more. These impacts are typically negative and can result in poor mental, emotional, physical, or financial health.

Similar to how you may go to the doctor for help with a physical ailment, addictions require professional support and appropriate care to achieve remission. Asking for that support is a sign of strength. If you think that you, or someone you know, might be struggling with addiction, please refer to the resources on page 162.

You Can Change Your Habits

You have now learned the fundamentals of habit change. You're doing great! With this information, you can achieve transformational results. By using CBT, Behavior Modification, and mindfulness techniques, you can intentionally leverage habits to reach your goals. Keep in mind that you will be taking small steps as you go. Therefore, consistency is key to obtaining the results you want. Take it step-by-step, little-by-little, and day-by-day.

In addition to the evidence-based techniques you are learning, remember to practice self-compassion. Even if you stumble on this journey, you can always get back up and begin again.

Being patient and kind toward yourself will help you continue to learn, grow, and thrive. Keep in mind that the habits you choose to introduce or eliminate should be in the service of your well-being.

You may face challenges during this process, as many of the teachings and techniques will be new to you. Challenges and setbacks are completely normal parts of the learning process. The challenge of creating positive habit change will be broken down into two steps: setting your goals and being systematic in your approach. Remember, it isn't about willpower; it's about clear goals, systems, and accountability.

Set Your Goals

Setting clear goals is key to creating and eliminating habits. Without goals, it would be extremely difficult to consistently build up and maintain healthy habits. There would be little motivation to keep going down the path of healthy habit change. Developing habits without clear goals in mind is like driving somewhere you've never been before without any directions. You may somehow end up at your desired destination, but it will take a lot longer and give you way more headaches! Goals are the road maps to creating a happy and healthy life. They give you clarity, direction, and purpose.

In this workbook, you will find concrete activities to help you. These tools will help you to better understand what your goals are and why they are important to you, as well as help you create a realistic program that will support you in achieving your goals.

Be Systematic and Self-Accountable

There are so many pieces and principles to habit change, which means it can feel overwhelming and intimidating to work toward new goals. But this workbook has you covered. The first step in this journey is to gain clarity on the outcomes you are seeking. Once you're clear on your goals, you will practice systems and accountability to help you achieve and maintain them. In this instance, consistent practice is key to success. There will be several exercises throughout this workbook to make this process manageable. Some examples of how you can be systematic and self-accountable include: building self-awareness, setting clear and attainable goals, monitoring your habits, and adapting tools to fit your unique needs. Don't forget that you are the expert of your own life, and this workbook is your supportive companion along the journey.

Key Takeaways

- Cognitive Behavioral Therapy (CBT) is a psychological area of study that looks at how thoughts, emotions, and behaviors influence each other. CBT techniques can help you add, strengthen, or eliminate habits.

- Behavior Modification aims to either increase or decrease certain behaviors (habits) using the behavior loop that consists of antecedent ➜ behavior ➜ consequence.

- Mindfulness can help you bring more awareness and intention to your daily habits. Mindfulness practices are also great habits to implement to improve your health and well-being.

- The techniques covered in this chapter can help you break down big goals into small actionable steps.

- Through goal-setting, systems, accountability, and consistency, you are capable of changing your habits and achieving your goals.

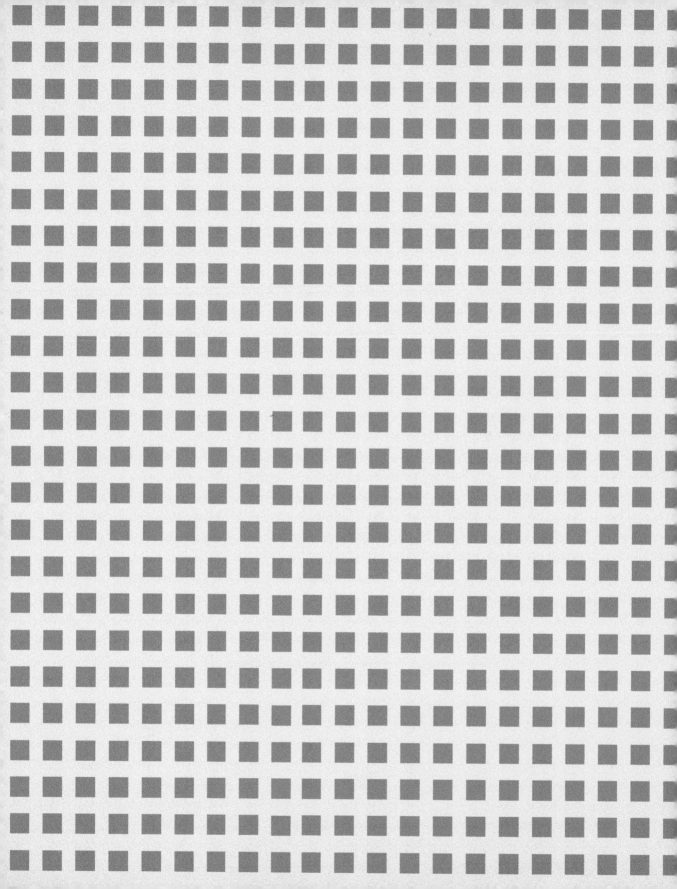

THE PATH TO SUCCESSFULLY CHANGING YOUR HABITS

n part II of this book, you will have the chance to reflect on, learn, and practice the various skills and tools for successfully changing your habits. You will find affirmations, prompts, practices, and exercises that will support you in finding clarity, getting unstuck, and identifying the right goals for you. In this section, you will work to identify your goals and uncover the habits required to achieve those goals. It is here that you will lay out the path to successfully changing and maintaining your habits and begin creating the changes you want in your life.

CHAPTER 3

Identify Your Goals

Have you ever attempted to reach a goal over and over again, but couldn't seem to get there? If so, you're not alone. Think of how many folks excitedly set the same resolution each New Year, only to give up before spring! It's not because they *can't* achieve their goals, but they likely lack the clarity needed to do so. This workbook will help show you how to approach goal-setting in a way that puts you on the path toward success.

With clarity, systems, and accountability, you can set and achieve goals with more confidence. In this chapter, you will strive to clearly identify and prioritize the goals you'll be working toward throughout the rest of the workbook. If you feel stuck, that's okay. The prompts, practices, and exercises will guide you through different ways to frame, evaluate, and begin working on your goals. It's time to get started!

Angel Finds Clarity and Consistency

Angel realized that he spent a lot of his day sitting down and that he often felt low on energy. He never had the energy to try new things or do activities with his family. In general, he felt dissatisfied with his health. Angel decided he wanted to be "healthier" and made this his goal. The problem? Angel wasn't certain what being "healthier" looked like for him.

He initially started by implementing many new habits at once. He decided to drink more water, exercise for an hour a day, and practice yoga. Angel found it hard to keep up. He was more exhausted than before! He knew he needed a better strategy. After learning about how setting the right goals could help him better succeed at achieving them, Angel decided he needed to clarify what "healthy" looked like for him. Angel decided that being healthier for him meant being more physically active. He began his changes slowly by going on a twenty-minute walk each morning while he drank his coffee. He made his morning coffee contingent on this walk. Soon, this walk became a consistent habit.

Angel used walking as the foundation for other healthy habits. He mindfully identified the best cues and rewards to keep him going. One cue he identified was finishing his lunch. After finishing lunch each day, he would go on a short walk as well. Even though Angel's goals were vague at first, he was able to use concrete strategies to make lifelong improvements to his health and happiness.

I AM CONSCIOUSLY CREATING GOALS THAT ALIGN WITH MY VALUES.

What are your values? What habits do you currently have that support or contradict these values? Your goals should reinforce your values, so getting clear on those values can help you identify the right goal.

What areas of your life would you like to improve? Identify desired changes for different aspects of your life, such as health, relationships, work, and hobbies.

GOALS AND HABITS INVENTORY QUIZ

Take a closer look at your current and past habits. This quiz will help you evaluate how these habits have impacted your past goals. After each statement, circle the number that most applies to you.

0 = Never, 1 = Rarely, 2 = Sometimes, 3 = Often, 4 = Almost Always, 5 = Always

I find it easy to initiate and maintain new habits.

0   1   2   3   4   5

I don't struggle to let go of unhealthy habits.

0   1   2   3   4   5

Procrastination doesn't keep me from achieving my goals.

0   1   2   3   4   5

I enjoy tracking my habits daily.

0   1   2   3   4   5

I enjoy working with someone who is willing to keep me accountable.

0   1   2   3   4   5

I enjoy working on my own.

0   1   2   3   4   5

If I put something on the calendar it will get done.

0   1   2   3   4   5

Researching how I can adopt a new habit is fun for me.

0   1   2   3   4   5

Prior to setting a new goal, I ask myself, "Why is this important to me?"

0   1   2   3   4   5

Prior to setting a new goal, I create a system to help me succeed.

0   1   2   3   4   5

I am confident in my abilities to start healthy habits and let go of unhealthy ones.

0   1   2   3   4   5

Scoring: Review your responses to the above statements. Take notice of the areas where you scored highly (4 to 5) and which scores were low (0 to 2). Do you notice any patterns? Are there strategies that work well for you? Are there areas you'd like to improve? Keep these answers in mind as you continue through this chapter.

REFLECTING ON YOUR PAST

A great way to set goals clearly and strategically is to reflect on how you've set goals in the past. Doing so gives you an opportunity to identify what's already working in your favor, and what approaches you want to change. Reflection is a key part of setting yourself up for success moving forward.

Respond thoughtfully to the questions below. You can also go through these talking points with a friend, family member, or colleague to gain additional insights. Or you can keep this reflection completely private.

What goals have I achieved that I am most proud of?

What are three personal or professional challenges I've overcome?

What lessons have I learned from my achievements and the obstacles I've overcome?

Are there any goals I tried to achieve in the past but was unable to? What stopped me?

_____

_____

_____

_____

What lessons have I learned from the goals I did not achieve?

_____

_____

_____

_____

What goals have I most enjoyed pursuing? What did I enjoy about the process?

_____

_____

_____

_____

To set myself up for success as I embark on my new goals, I will:

_____

_____

_____

_____

Mindful Breathing

A great way to develop your mindfulness skills is by learning to be mindful of your breath. Your breathing can signal if you are relaxed or stressed. Conversely, changing your breathing can also help you change your emotional state.

Your breath can be a great anchor to ground you at any moment. Use the following steps to help you practice mindful breathing:

1. Begin by taking notice of your breathing without judgment. Don't make any changes for now. Are you breathing from your chest or your stomach? Is your breath shallow or deep? Slow or fast? Notice the current state of your breath for about one minute.

2. Lightly place one hand onto your stomach. Begin breathing deeply so that your stomach slowly inflates like a balloon. Feel your hand rise as your stomach rises. Breathe out and feel your hand fall as your stomach falls. Repeat this three times, bringing your full attention to the rising and falling of your hand on your stomach.

3. On the next in-breath, breathe in for a count of five. Then hold your breath for a count of five. Breathe out for a count of five. Then hold your breath for a count of five. Repeat this sequence five times while keeping your hand lightly on your stomach.

4. Notice how this change in breath makes you feel. Are you more relaxed? More focused? Is your body more or less tense? Take your time noticing any changes without judging them as good or bad.

5. Whenever you are ready, you can release your hand from your stomach. You may resume your normal breathing. Take note of any positive effects this exercise had. You can implement this mindful breathing strategy anytime you want to ground yourself and connect with your breath.

Reflect on your values and desired areas of change. What is one goal you can set related to your values and desired change?

What does a successful outcome look and feel like? How would your life be different? Be specific to help you evaluate your goal along the way.

Meditate on the Outcome

It can be a bit overwhelming to pick a goal. Your mind can be full of conflicting thoughts, feelings, and questions that make the process challenging. Meditating on the desired outcome can provide clarity on how to get there.

Follow these simple steps to meditate on your outcome and gain clarity on the right goal:

1. Find a comfortable space where you can sit in a supported position. Take a moment to settle in and find stillness.

2. Take three long and slow deep breaths, with your out-breaths being twice as long as your in-breaths. You can repeat these as needed.

3. Close your eyes if you feel comfortable. If not, find a fixed point and soften your gaze as you look at it.

4. Ask yourself, "One year from now, how would I like to feel?" Notice the words that come to mind (such as confident, peaceful, or joyous). Don't censor yourself.

5. Meditate on your feelings. Imagine the feelings moving through your body in a pleasant way.

6. Ask yourself, "What can I do to feel this way?" Is it finding a new job? Enjoying more quality time with friends? Creating art? Again, trust the answers you receive and do not censor yourself.

7. Take three more deep and slow breaths before gently opening your eyes.

Now that you are clear on how you want to feel, and the potential routes to achieve this, pick a goal that aligns with those two factors to get started on your goal-setting journey.

REVISIT THE BRAIN-DUMP

It can be challenging to know where to get started with your goals. But you're already farther ahead than you may realize.

In chapter 1, you did a brain-dump of ideas for goals (page 11). You then reviewed all of the ideas and grouped them into life sectors. In this exercise, you will list the top five goals that you feel most motivated to achieve. You will select one goal from five of the following areas of life: relationships, work, health, spirituality, and self-care. You can also swap out any of these categories for ones that resonate more with you. This will provide you with a concrete visual representation of the goals you will prioritize moving forward.

Category 1: _____

Goal: _____

Category 2: _____

Goal: _____

Category 3: _____

Goal: _____

Category 4: _____

Goal: _____

Category 5: _____

Goal: _____

SET S.M.A.R.T. GOALS

Now that you've identified the general goals you'd like to work on, use the S.M.A.R.T. acronym to help shape them into something you can work on concretely. This acronym stands for **s**pecific, **m**easurable, **a**chievable, **r**elevant, and **t**ime-bound.

Fill out the following prompts for one of the goals you're working on.

Goal:

Specific: Make your goals specific for effective planning. For example, a vague goal is, "I want to eat healthier." What does "healthier" look like? A specific goal is, "I will eat healthier by having vegetables with at least two meals per day."

Measurable: How will you know if your efforts are successful? Is there a concrete point at which you know you've achieved your goal? Identify how you will measure success.

Achievable: Consider how achievable this goal is. You want the goal to challenge you, but you also want to set yourself up for success. What is a specific habit you will implement to achieve this goal?

Relevant: How relevant is this goal to your current lifestyle? Does it connect to your relationships or professional development? Identify how this goal is relevant.

Time-bound: When a goal is restricted to a fixed time frame, you are more likely to achieve it. Is your goal long-term or short-term? From there you can set milestones along the way to keep you on track. Identify those milestones here.

HOW TO PRIORITIZE MULTIPLE GOALS

Prioritizing your goals is an important part of actually reaching them. To effectively prioritize your goals, you need to assess several elements, such as urgency and impact. Urgent goals are time-sensitive and have an upcoming "due date." Impactful goals should align with your long-term vision and values. By learning to weigh and prioritize urgency and impact, you'll be able to set and achieve goals with more clarity and ease.

For this exercise, complete the following steps to help you prioritize your goals:

1. List your goals from the **Revisit the Brain-Dump** exercise on page 39:

    * _____

    * _____

    * _____

    * _____

    * _____

2. Place each goal into their appropriate space in the table on the following page based on the Eisenhower Matrix, a task management tool. Remember: Urgency refers to how time-sensitive a goal is, and impact is based on how important you believe the goal is to your long-term life aspirations and values.

	URGENT	NOT URGENT
HIGH IMPACT	*Urgent and Important*	*Not Urgent and Important*
LOW IMPACT	*Urgent and Not Important*	*Not Urgent and Not Important*

3. You now have a visual representation of which goals are both time-sensitive and impactful in your life. You can get started by prioritizing the goals that are both urgent and impactful. If you placed any goals under the not urgent and not impactful sector, you can decide whether or not you would like to adjust those goals or eliminate them all together.

4. Remember to remain flexible. The urgency and impact of these goals may change over time, and that's okay. You can reorder your goals, or even drop goals that no longer align with your values, as needed.

Your Environment
and Your Goals

Environment influences your behaviors. As you set out to achieve your goals, you want to be in a supportive environment. Once you've identified the first goal you would like to focus on, take a look at the spaces where you spend the majority of your time. This could be a living room, desk at work, car, or anywhere else you spend a lot of your time. Pretend like you are seeing the space for the first time.

Keep your goal in mind as you objectively observe the environment. Now ask yourself, "Does this environment support or inhibit my goal? Are there any easy changes I can make to support my goal?"

For example, if your goal is to journal every morning, look at where you spend most of your time in the morning (bedroom, kitchen table, etc.) and identify a spot where you can keep a journal and pen handy. If you see your journal and pen in that environment every morning, it is much more likely you will use them!

How can you adapt your environment to support each of your goals? Make it happen!

SHAPE YOUR ENVIRONMENT FOR SUCCESS

After you've taken time to observe your environments mindfully and objectively, you can shape them to support your goals. For example, if your goal is to read twenty-four books in a year, and the habit you've selected to support this goal is reading each morning, then you can adjust your environment by placing the book you're currently reading on your nightstand. This makes it so that one of the first things you see when you wake up is the book, and it's easily within arm's reach for you to pick up and engage in your habit. Conversely, if your goal is to eliminate a habit such as eating cookies before bed, you can alter your kitchen environment so that the cookies are either extremely inconvenient to reach (i.e., on a high shelf) or removed from your home altogether.

Identify adjustments you can make to your environment to support your habits and goals by breaking them down into categories. Write out ideas for shaping your environment for success in each category provided below; there is also space for you to add in an additional category as needed.

ENVIRONMENT	ADJUSTMENTS
Bedroom	
Living Room	
Kitchen	
Bathroom	
Car/Transportation	
Workspace	

Connect with Someone Who Will Support You

You don't have to go through this goal-setting journey alone. In addition to this workbook, you can find clarity and support from people you know and who support your efforts. Humans are social creatures, and it can add more fun to the process if you engage others.

Think of someone in your life that you know, like, and who will be supportive of your efforts. Reach out to that person and let them know you're in the process of setting new goals. Ask if they can give you some objective feedback on areas where you may be stuck.

When it comes to asking others for their help and opinions, it's important to clearly communicate expectations. Do you want to talk or text? Let them know if you're just looking for someone to hear you out while you think aloud, or if you want them to ask you clarifying questions. Remember, this practice is meant to be fun and help build your support system as you form healthy habits and reach for your goals. Give it a try with as many people as you want in your support system.

Turning Off Autopilot and Turning On Your Five Senses

If you feel stuck or disconnected from your goals, it's possible you are living on autopilot—just going about your tasks automatically, without really being engaged. To help turn off the sensation of being on autopilot, you can focus your attention on your available senses.

For this practice, it can be helpful to go outside or be near a window if possible. Being in or near nature can make the practice easier. Sit comfortably, stand, or lie down in stillness. Relax your breath and body as much as possible. Next, mentally identify one-by-one what you're experiencing using your available senses.

You will likely notice things you had not noticed before. This is good! It means you are engaging with the present moment. Use this practice anytime you notice feeling stuck and/or like you're on autopilot. As you reengage with your available senses, it will feel easier to take intentional action toward your goals.

Mindful Visualization of Your Future Self

Taking a moment to pause and visualize yourself after you've reached your goal can provide you with clarity and inspiration.

   Complete the following steps to mindfully visualize the outcome of your goal:

1. Find a comfortable space to sit in a supported position. Take a moment to settle in and find stillness.

2. Take three long and slow deep breaths, with your out-breaths being twice as long as your in-breaths. You can repeat these as needed.

3. Notice any tension you may be holding in your body and gently release it. Make sure your jaw is unclenched and your shoulders are relaxed.

4. Close your eyes or find a fixed point to focus on as you soften your gaze. Now imagine yourself after you've achieved your goal. How do you look? What expression is on your face? What problems have been resolved? How do you spend your time? How are you living your values? Soak in this visualization using all of your available senses.

5. Notice any positive thoughts, emotions, or sensations that come up as you visualize your future self. Allow the positivity to grow and expand in your mind and body.

6. Whenever you're ready, you can slowly open your eyes and take another deep and slow breath. Repeat this visualization as needed to help you realign with your goal and find inspiration.

IDENTIFY YOUR "WHY" CHECKLIST

Understanding the "why" behind your goals is key to staying consistent, especially when you run into roadblocks.

Take some time to look over the provided checklist of common reasons people set goals and embark on healthier habits. Check off any of the reasons that apply to you and your goals. There is space to add additional reasons. Whenever you're feeling stuck or need a motivational boost, refer back to this checklist.

☐ To have more energy

☐ To spend more time with loved ones

☐ To live a long and healthy life

☐ To stop procrastinating

☐ To manage my stress

☐ To improve my financial well-being

☐ To stop feeling distracted

☐ To boost my creativity

☐ To grow professionally

☐ To have healthier relationships

☐ To connect more deeply with others

☐ To be more organized

☐ To relax in healthy ways

☐ To master a certain skill or talent

☐ To learn a new skill

☐ To feel confident in my _____

(body/abilities/relationships)

☐ _____

_____

☐ _____

_____

☐ _____

_____

Key Takeaways

- Reflecting on past habits and goals can give you crucial information to plan for future goals.

- Identifying your values can help you set the right goals.

- Mindfulness can help you feel grounded and set goals that align with your values and desires.

- An effective goal is S.M.A.R.T.: **s**pecific, **m**easurable, **a**chievable, **r**elevant, and **t**ime-bound.

CHAPTER 4

Uncover the Habits to Achieve Your Goals

Now that you've clearly identified your goals, it's time to figure out what habit changes you'll need in order to get started on achieving them. In this chapter, you'll find various tools designed to help you uncover which habits you will be releasing and which ones you'll be intentionally building. You will utilize prompts to help you reflect, and use a mixture of practices and exercises to decipher which habits need changing and which habits you want to build.

If you need additional motivation, go back to the affirmation (page 31) and repeat it regularly. As you've already seen throughout this workbook, habit change is not an overnight process. It requires mindfulness, strategy, and consistency. The great news is that you're already actively working on these elements through the pages of this book. Remember, when working on the following tools, you can refer back to the goals you identified in chapter 3. It's time to get started!

Ayla Learns the Power of Monitoring

Ayla set a goal to run in a charitable 10k race. This goal aligned with her values of living an active life and giving back to her community. She gave herself twelve weeks to train. However, day after day Ayla struggled to meet her training goals. She felt stuck and uncertain about how to reach her goal.

Ayla turned to her girlfriend Sarah for advice because Sarah seemed to easily reach many of her goals. She felt that Sarah would be good support for her. Sarah suggested that Ayla focus on her habits first. Ayla reviewed her current habits and recognized potential areas of change. For example, Ayla noted she was going to bed late and, therefore, missing her morning runs. She identified that the first step in achieving her goal would be to develop the habit of going to bed earlier. With her commitment to this single habit, she was able to wake up for her morning runs.

Sarah also helped Ayla create a habit tracker. Every day that Ayla trained for the race she would check a box. Ayla loved the visual representation of her progress and looked forward to it. Lastly, to help stay motivated every day, Ayla repeated the affirmation, "I am able to achieve my goal one step at a time."

Overall, having social support, changing a current habit, tracking her new habit, and repeating an affirmation helped Ayla achieve her goal. With the right habits in place, she was able to complete her 10k race with confidence and ease.

I AM CAPABLE OF RELEASING
AND CREATING HABITS TO HELP ME
ACHIEVE MY GOALS.

Are there any unhealthy habits you've been able to eliminate in the past? What did you need to do in order to let go of those habits (e.g., awareness, mindset, concrete steps)? Analyzing how you've successfully let go of bad habits, no matter how big or small the habits were, can give you useful insights. Identify any lessons that you may be able to apply to current bad habits.

_____

_____

_____

_____

What are some favorite healthy habits that you've adopted? Why do you enjoy these habits? Where did these habits come from? Since habits are by nature automatic, it can be hard to recognize which habits are already providing you benefits. Focusing on what is already working, and why it works, can help you figure out which new habits you'd like to implement. Look at your current habits with fresh eyes to gain objective insights.

_____

_____

_____

_____

Habit Body Scan

Conducting a body scan will help you develop insights into how a habit impacts your physical body. It can be used for good or bad habits.

Select a habit that you'd like to bring more awareness to.

Habit: _____

_____

The next time you do the selected habit follow this practice:

1. Close your eyes if you want.

2. Take note of what's happening in your body.

3. Bring awareness to your posture and how your body is positioned.

4. Begin at the top of your head, and slowly bring awareness downward until you reach the tips of your toes.

5. Notice, without judgment, if there are any areas of tension. If you don't feel anything at all right now, that's okay. Continue staying engaged.

6. Bring your awareness to your breath. Take note of whether your breathing is fast, slow, shallow, or deep. Does this breath feel comfortable to you? Do not change anything, just notice.

7. Once you've fully scanned your body and connected with your breath, take three slow and long deep breaths. If your eyes are closed, you may open them.

What new insights do you have about this habit after assessing how it affects your body?

_____

_____

_____

HEALTHY HABITS BRAINSTORM LIST

If you're struggling to identify healthy or good habits to practice, this is a helpful exercise to get you started.

Below you'll find a checklist of fifteen potential healthy habits followed by additional blank spaces. Read through the list, and then add your own ideas for healthy habits that come to mind. Once you've completed the list, read it back to yourself. As you reread the list, you can check off the healthy habits you would like to implement. The listed habits can be daily, weekly, or monthly.

Take your time with this exercise to increase your mindfulness as you identify the correct habits for you.

☐ Plan my meals for the week

☐ Call a loved one once per week

☐ Read one book per month

☐ Meditate for five minutes a day

☐ Log my water intake daily

☐ Check in with my goals monthly

☐ Eat a balanced breakfast
each morning

☐ Spend time in nature once per week

☐ Take medications daily

☐ Schedule my upcoming week

☐ Do one act of kindness per day

☐ Stretch every night before bed

☐ Go to a fitness class or group once
per week

☐ Clean my home once per week

☐ Get seven to eight hours of sleep
each night

☐ _____

☐ _____

☐ _____

☐ _____

☐ _____

☐ _____

☐ _____

Habits and Affirmations

Affirmations are positive statements that help you manage negative thoughts and beliefs. Affirmations are often repeated over a period of time (a day, a week, or longer) to help solidify the positive belief. You can use affirmations to help increase your confidence, boost focus, and overcome limiting beliefs about yourself. Affirmations can bolster healthy habits and can become healthy habits themselves. For example, you can make a goal to replace negative self-talk or self-sabotaging behaviors with repeating positive affirmations.

Think of one to three affirmations about habits for yourself. What would you like to feel and believe during this process? Once you've identified affirmations that feel right for you, repeat them silently or aloud to yourself each day for the next week.

Think about some of your current habits (e.g., morning cup of coffee, stretching before bed, biting your nails). How do these habits bring you closer to or farther away from achieving the goals you've decided to work on?

Pick one bad habit you'd like to eliminate. What reward do you gain from doing this bad habit? What potential healthy habits could give you a similar reward? Remember, the reason you likely continue doing bad habits isn't that you lack willpower, but because they fulfill a need you have. Gaining clarity on what that need is can help you eventually replace the habit with a healthier one.

Mindful Awareness of Current Habits

As you uncover the habits to achieve your goals, it's important to be mindful of the dozens of habits you already have in place. This awareness informs if you need to make any habit changes and what those changes may look like. You may discover you have habits you were not consciously aware of.

Pick an upcoming day that is a typical day in your life. Make a commitment that you will be more mindful of your habits for the entire day. At this time, you don't need to judge or adjust any habits. This is about raising your awareness. Since this level of awareness is likely new, it can be helpful to set up reminders for yourself throughout the day. You can set alarms, add prompts to your calendar, or put up sticky notes around your space. These reminders will signal for you to pause and check-in with your habits.

Helpful questions to ask yourself during this practice include:

- What's the first thing I do when I get out of bed?

- What time do I have my first meal?

- Do I struggle to find things throughout the day?

- How often do I get up and move?

- How do I begin to wind down for bed?

Habits and Movement

One category of habits that is important to achieving a variety of goals is movement. Movement looks different for each person depending on ability, resources, and time, but provides you with benefits in many areas of life. According to the Mayo Clinic, regular body movement can improve health, productivity, and overall life satisfaction. Therefore, movement can support other habits and goals and, at the same time, be a habit on its own.

If becoming healthier is a goal for you, a daily habit of twenty minutes of movement can be a great place to start. If producing more positivity in your life is a goal, dancing to your favorite song whenever you are sad can help boost endorphins and your mood. Consider potential small habits you could adopt to increase movement based on your abilities. What are things you can do to move more than you already do? Here are some possibilities of small habits to foster movement in your life:

- Commit to always using the stairs.

- Take your pet for a twenty-minute walk once per day.

- Set a reminder to stretch once per day.

- Use a standing desk when possible.

- Ask your physician for safe, gentle movements you can do daily.

- Take calls while moving around your home.

Once you've selected the types of movement habits you'd like to start, consider how long you'd like to move, at what time of day, and how often to help make implementing these habits more achievable.

HABITS THROUGHOUT THE DAY

Habits are often linked to specific times of the day. Increasing awareness of these habits, both good and bad, can help you identify what's already working and what, if any, changes need to be made. Take time to reflect on the habits you do at different points in the day and see if you notice any patterns. Do most of your healthy habits happen in the morning? Do you have less concrete habits in the afternoon? How are your evening habits related to your energy levels? To deepen your understanding, respond to the following prompts:

The first habit I have when I wake up each morning is:

My morning habits usually include:

My morning habits make me feel:

My afternoon habits usually include:

_____

_____

_____

My afternoon habits make me feel:

_____

_____

_____

My nighttime habits usually include:

_____

_____

_____

My nighttime habits make me feel:

_____

_____

_____

The last habit I do before going to bed is:

_____

_____

_____

Identify Your Habit Support System

Having a support system as you embark on habit change can help you remain motivated and consistent. Your support system can provide you with accountability, encouragement, and a fresh perspective.

Think about the people you are close to among your loved ones, social groups, or colleagues. Reflect on the following questions to solidify your habit support system:

- Does anyone in your inner circle have habits you admire?

- How do the people you've identified typically support you?

- Do any of the people you've identified have similar goals?

- Are you able to ask someone to be your accountability partner for a specific habit?

You can reach out to folks from your goal-support system, or communicate with an entirely new group of people. The key to developing a habit support system is finding folks that you feel comfortable with and supported by.

HABITS AND STRESS

A common objective of habit change is to reduce stress. You can accomplish this by eliminating habits that create stress and implementing habits that reduce it.

Use this form to track how certain habits impact your stress levels. Note the time and place where you engage in a habit; your stress level, on a scale from 1 (low) to 5 (high), prior to engaging in the habit; and your stress level after completing the habit.

HABIT	TIME/PLACE	STRESS LEVEL BEFORE (1 TO 5)	STRESS LEVEL AFTER (1 TO 5)

Mindful Consumption Practice

What you consume, including food, drinks, television, media, music, books, etc., significantly influences the habits you develop. Mindful consumption can help you be more aware of your habits and support you in creating healthy ones.

A great way to begin a mindful consumption practice is by slowing down. Slow down when you eat. Slow down when you're purchasing items. Slow down when selecting what media to engage with. Even if it feels silly at first to do things slowly, it's an easy first step to noticing what you're consuming and why you're consuming it. Pick an area of your life (e.g., eating, shopping, getting ready in the morning) and commit to doing those tasks more slowly for the next week. See what you notice about how and why you consume things. Then, try slowing things down in another area of your life and repeating this process. What do you notice about your habits when you slow things down?

POSITIVE HABITS CALENDAR

A fun way to try out a variety of positive habits is to use a habits calendar. The objective is to leverage simple habits to improve your well-being. Additionally, it gives you the chance to try out different habits.

   This calendar will prompt you to complete one positive behavior per day for twenty-eight days. Feel free to swap out any behaviors in the calendar for your own ideas. You can try doing all the habits each day for the twenty-eight days or try one new behavior each day. In either case, be mindful and consider which ones you want to continue doing.

MON	TUE	WED	THURS	FRI	SAT	SUN
Set aside three minutes for a mindfulness exercise.	Reach out to a friend or loved one.	Take time to reflect on your values.	Spend ten minutes outside.	Review your progress on one of your S.M.A.R.T. goals.	Complete a body scan to check in with yourself.	Take a break from technology.
Visualize yourself achieving your goals.	Move your body in a way that feels good.	Repeat a positive affirmation to yourself three times.	Journal about something you're grateful for.	Ask someone you trust to be your accountability buddy for one habit.	Pick a mundane activity and commit to doing it mindfully.	Make a list of goals you've achieved in your life so far.
Review your progress on another S.M.A.R.T. goal.	Ask for help today.	Slow down one of your habits to increase mindfulness.	Make a list of habits you currently have that you are proud of.	Reflect on three things you are grateful for.	Stretch for five minutes.	Celebrate your efforts to change your habits.
Thank yourself for committing to positive habit change.	Make time for play today.	Take a break and prioritize rest.	Reconnect with your "why" for your current goals.	Do a small favor to make someone else's day easier.	Make your environment more conducive for your desirable habit.	Do something that feels good for your body and mind.

BREAK A BAD HABIT

A bad habit is any habit that negatively impacts your goals, relationships, health, and well-being. You likely continue to engage in bad habits because they provide you with short-term rewards. For example, biting your nails may temporarily reduce stress. Ideally, you can replace bad habits with better ones that provide similar rewards without the negative consequences. Instead of biting your nails to relieve stress, you could take three deep breaths.

   Identify three bad habits you want to break. Beneath each bad habit, list potential good habits you could replace them with. You can refer back to your list of substitutes as often as you need until the bad habit has been fully replaced.

A habit I want to break: _____

Positive replacement habit: _____

Positive replacement habit: _____

Positive replacement habit: _____

A habit I want to break: _____

Positive replacement habit: _____

Positive replacement habit: _____

Positive replacement habit: _____

A habit I want to break: _____

Positive replacement habit: _____

Positive replacement habit: _____

Positive replacement habit: _____

BREAKING DOWN GOALS INTO HABITS

A key component of successfully reaching your goals is to break each goal down into smaller habits that support that goal. This provides you with concrete ways to define your goal and track your progress. This exercise will help you in breaking down goals into habits.

In the previous chapter, you identified one goal from five different areas of focus in your life (page 42). In this exercise, you will break down three of those goals further by listing out five potential habits that could help you achieve that goal. You can even list a habit you want to break and cross it out. This will help you begin to connect your habits with your goals. It's okay if your target habits change as you continue through this workbook; use this exercise as a space to start putting your ideas to paper.

Goal 1: _____

Habit: _____

Habit: _____

Habit: _____

Goal 2: _____

Habit: _____

Habit: _____

Habit: _____

Goal 3: _____

Habit: _____

Habit: _____

Habit: _____

TRACK YOUR HABITS

One of the most effective ways to remain consistent with a habit is to track how often you do it. Using a habit tracker is a simple way to measure how often you do (or don't do) a selected habit. A habit tracker creates a visual reminder to engage in your habit. It also provides a sense of accomplishment when you are able to mark down that you did the habit you wanted to.

You can use the habit tracker in this exercise for one or multiple habits you would like to monitor over a 30-day period.

DAILY HABITS	1	2	3	4	5	6	7	8	9	10
Example: 8 hours of sleep										

11	12	13	14	15	16	17	18	19	20	21	22	23	24	25	26	27	28	29	30

Key Takeaways

■ Habits (daily, weekly, monthly) are the building blocks of achieving your goals.

■ Increasing mindful awareness of your habits is the first step to figuring out what habits you want to change, release, or implement.

■ You can lean on social supports and affirmations to stay motivated as you change your habits.

■ Visual representations help you monitor your habits and remain consistent.

CHAPTER 5

Use CBT-Based Tools

You've already learned the background and foundation of Cognitive Behavioral Therapy (CBT) in a previous chapter. In this chapter, you will discover how to use CBT techniques to initiate and sustain behavior change. This includes starting new habits, maintaining those habits, and ultimately reaching your goals. The following prompts, practices, and exercises will help you understand the connections between your thoughts, emotions, and behaviors (habits) in a more mindful manner.

You will be guided through the tools that can help you challenge negative thoughts, reflect, and create sustainable positive habits. In essence, at the end of this chapter, you will be equipped with researched techniques to support you in intentionally reaching your goals through positive habits. Remain open to trying out each of these techniques so that you can fully understand what works best for you.

Yuna Breaks Free

Yuna was studying design and had a lot of responsibilities. She would take classes and go to work during the day. In the evenings she wanted to work on her designs, but she developed the habit of watching television instead. She was often stressed, and watching TV distracted her. However, each night she'd watch TV for hours, and, as a result, she didn't have time to work on her designs. Yuna set a goal to break the habit of watching TV. She wanted more time to work on her designs and to align her goals with her value of creativity.

Yuna began by noticing the thought she had right before she turned on the television each night. As soon as she'd get home from a busy day, her thought was, "I'm too tired to do anything." She recognized that the thought made her feel more exhausted, and she would lay on the couch and turn on her television. The recognition of this pattern helped Yuna see what needed to change.

She decided that when she had the thought, "I'm too tired to do anything," she would take a three-minute mindfulness break instead of turning on the television. This small check-in helped Yuna feel more relaxed. Over time she watched less television, some days not watching any at all. She had more time to work on her designs and express her creativity. In this way, Yuna used a simple, yet effective, CBT technique to help her break free from the television slump and reach her goals.

I CAN CREATE LASTING CHANGE IN MY LIFE BY CHANGING MY THOUGHTS AND ACTIONS.

What negative thoughts have you recently had about yourself or others? How have these thoughts made you feel? How have you been behaving in response to these thoughts and feelings?

_____

_____

_____

_____

_____

_____

What is a positive thought you would like to believe about yourself? For example, "I am a considerate friend." What habits can you practice that align with this positive thought—for example, the habit of calling your friends to see how they are doing? How would you feel about yourself after engaging in these habits?

_____

_____

_____

_____

_____

_____

NOTICE YOUR NEGATIVE THOUGHTS

Everyone experiences negative thoughts from time to time, but frequent automatic negative statements can impact your feelings and your subsequent ability to engage in healthy habits. In order to change negative thoughts, you must first become aware of them. This checklist provides some common negative thoughts that people have. Check off those thoughts you are prone to thinking. You may also add in any negative thoughts you frequently have that are not listed. This awareness will help you quickly and clearly identify negative thoughts so that you can work on changing them in any of the ways detailed in this book, such as in **Plan for Positive Thoughts** (page 89), **Challenge the Worst-Case Scenario** (page 87), and **Fact-Check Your Thoughts** (page 79).

- ☐ I am not good enough.

- ☐ I will always be in this negative situation.

- ☐ I got the promotion because I was lucky.

- ☐ I should have accomplished more by my age.

- ☐ If I am not doing well at everything, I am a failure.

- ☐ I will never stick with my habits consistently.

- ☐ I feel like a failure; therefore, I am a failure.

- ☐ Everybody else feels confident; I am the only one who does not.

- ☐ If I was smarter, I'd be more successful.

- ☐ I should put other people's needs before my own.

- ☐ I received a good review at work, but the one negative comment is what matters.

- ☐ My friends don't think I am interesting; it's a fluke that they spend time with me.

- ☐ I will give up now before I inevitably fail.

- ☐ I should be able to do this task better.

- ☐ Either people like me, or they hate me.

- ☐ I should be more like other people in my life and less like myself.

- ☐ _____

- ☐ _____

FACT-CHECK YOUR THOUGHTS

Many people tend to believe that the thoughts they have are inherently true. But in reality, your thoughts are not facts. Although some thoughts you have might be factual ("I didn't work out today"), others are not factual ("I am lazy"). When you confuse your thoughts for facts, it can lead to a lack of motivation and a desire to engage in unhealthy habits. Therefore, it's crucial to distinguish opinions from facts.

Use this exercise to practice distinguishing facts and opinions by reading the thought and checking the correct box. Use the last two blank spaces to write in negative thought patterns you've noticed you have and check whether they are fact or opinion.

Thought	Fact	Opinion
1. I failed the test.	☐	☐
2. I am dumb.	☐	☐
3. I forgot to pay the bill.	☐	☐
4. I am irresponsible.	☐	☐
5. I am not good at anything.	☐	☐
6. I dislike my current job.	☐	☐
7. I am awkward and unlikeable.	☐	☐
8. I had an awkward interaction with someone today.	☐	☐
9. I never do anything right.	☐	☐
10. I make mistakes just like everybody else.	☐	☐
11. _____	☐	☐
12. _____	☐	☐

What habits do you already have that help you have positive thoughts and feelings? How can you use these habits when you are experiencing negative thoughts and feelings?

What is one potential barrier to achieving one of your goals? Is there another way you can look at this barrier so it feels less daunting? Are there steps you can take to address this barrier when it arises?

Challenge the Idea of "Perfect"

Consider how the concept of doing your habits "perfectly" may be limiting your progress. Sometimes you may not be able to do your habits perfectly due to low energy, time constraints, or other factors. That's okay! You can still do something to engage with your habit and get you closer to your goals. For example, say you are working on the habit of reading for twenty minutes each day, but one day you are too tired to read for a full twenty minutes. Instead, you could read five minutes that day, which is more progress than not reading at all. It is consistency that creates habits.

For this practice, challenge the idea of "perfect" and adjust your habits as needed to help you stay consistent. Is there a habit you tend to skip if you can't do it perfectly? Start there!

After you've acted, even when it's not perfect, don't forget to congratulate yourself and acknowledge your progress. For example, if you're trying to develop the habit of doing a sixty-second plank, but can only manage thirty seconds, then do thirty seconds! After you've completed your thirty-second plank, congratulate yourself for staying consistent and engaging in your habit.

LOG YOUR THOUGHTS

A great way to understand the connection between your own thoughts, feelings, and actions is by using a thought log. Use this model to log and reflect on a variety of situations—from positive to negative, big to small.

This exercise gives you the space to explore your experiences and better understand your resulting thoughts, feelings, and behaviors. First, identify an area where you'd like to clarify and possibly change your thoughts, feelings, and behaviors. For example, if you are attempting to eliminate the habit of gossiping, but one day you gossiped at lunch with friends, you can use this thought log to better understand why you reengaged in gossip by objectively looking at the situation and your subsequent reactions. Once you've completed your written responses in this exercise, take time to reread your answers and reflect on any connections or new insights you've had.

The situation that happened:

The thoughts you had about this situation were:

The feelings that arose for you were:

_____

_____

_____

_____

The actions you took in response to your thoughts and emotions were:

_____

_____

_____

_____

_____

Some insights you've gained from reflecting on this experience are:

_____

_____

_____

_____

_____

Three Minutes of Mindfulness Check-In

A large part of having success with CBT techniques depends on your ability to mindfully check in with your thoughts, feelings, actions, and body. This check-in is a mindfulness practice you can do to strengthen your ability to observe these factors.

Similar to other mindfulness practices, if repeated consistently, this practice can become a positive habit in its own right. Do each of the following three steps for one minute each:

1. Observe your present experience. Where are you? What are you doing? What senses do you notice?

2. Identify your current emotion(s). Are you sad? Are you anxious? Are you excited? Are you hopeful?

3. Attend to your physical needs. Do you need to take a break, stretch, get water, eat, or use the bathroom? Take one minute to attend to your physical needs.

Schedule Mindfulness Breaks

In order to support effective behavior change, it's important to be mindful of your mental, emotional, and physical needs throughout the day.

Schedule mindfulness breaks to check in with yourself. During these check-ins, you can utilize any of the mindfulness techniques you've learned, such as mindful breathing, visualization, and body scans. If it's helpful, you can schedule these breaks in your calendar to help you remember. You can also make an agreement with an accountability partner to remind each other to take mindfulness breaks. Aim for three mindfulness breaks each day.

Grounding for Difficult Feelings

Experiencing difficult emotions is a normal part of life. Unfortunately, the times when you feel difficult emotions are when it's most tempting to revert to bad habits to distract you from what you're feeling. Practicing a grounding technique can help you focus on something other than the challenging emotion without engaging in an unhealthy habit. Grounding is a way of centering yourself in the present moment and practicing healthy detachment to help you gain control of thoughts, feelings, and behaviors.

Follow this prompt to practice grounding:

1. Pause what you are doing and observe the environment around you.

2. Describe the environment in detail (if you feel comfortable, do this aloud). Notice colors, textures, sounds, smells, and light around you. For example: "I see one white table, two brown chairs, and a shaggy gray rug. I can hear cars outside the open window . . ."

3. Continue this process of observing and objectively describing your environment for as long as needed until you begin to feel calm.

Challenge the Worst-Case Scenario

When changing your habits and working toward goals, it's normal to feel intimidated. You may have negative thoughts that the worst-case scenario will occur. For example, you may have the negative thought, "I will never reach my goal and will look silly for trying." Negative thoughts may prevent you from engaging in your healthy habits because you think the worst is inevitable. Challenging your negative thoughts can help you to see things more objectively and engage in behaviors that support your goals.

Answer these questions (in your head or aloud) to challenge worst-case scenario thoughts:

- What am I worried might happen?

- How likely is it that the worst-case scenario will come true?

- How likely is it that the worst-case scenario won't come true?

- If the worst did happen, what could I do to cope?

- Is there an affirmation I can repeat to give myself reassurance?

YOUR OWN COGNITIVE TRIANGLE

One of the key concepts of CBT is the cognitive triangle. This is a visual representation of the interplay between thoughts, emotions, and behaviors. A situation is any event that happens in your life that initiates the cognitive triangle. This means that when you change your thoughts about a situation, you can also change your emotions and behaviors.

Think of a situation you regularly encounter and that you'd like to change your reactions to. Fill out the elements of the cognitive triangle depicting how you would typically respond. Next, fill out the second cognitive triangle planning out how you'd like to respond instead.

Situation: _____

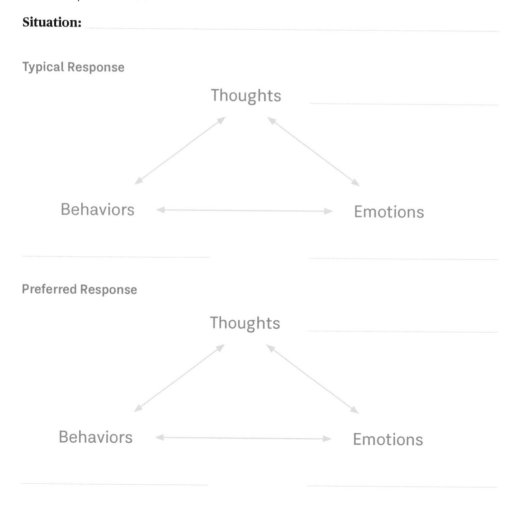

Typical Response

Thoughts _____

Behaviors ⟷ Emotions

_____   _____

Preferred Response

Thoughts _____

Behaviors ⟷ Emotions

_____   _____

Plan for Positive Thoughts

It is normal to experience negative thoughts about yourself, others, and circumstances. But when you begin to repeat and believe your negative thoughts, they have adverse effects on your emotions and behaviors. For example, if you were to think, "I always say the wrong thing," over and over, you may feel ashamed (emotion) and withdraw from the people in your life (behavior). This cycle can make it difficult for you to reach your goal of spending more quality time with others. In lieu of getting stuck in a negative cycle, you can identify positive thoughts to replace the negative ones.

Begin by identifying one negative thought you often repeat to yourself. Then identify a positive thought to replace it. Each time you catch yourself thinking or saying the negative statement, gently remind yourself of the positive one instead. For example, instead of "I always say the wrong thing," you can say to yourself, "I am improving my communication skills."

POSITIVE THOUGHTS, EMOTIONS, AND HABITS LOG

Keeping track of the positive thoughts, emotions, and habits you engage in each day can help you see how far you've come.

Once a day, set aside a couple of minutes to write down one positive thought you had, one positive emotion you felt, and one healthy habit you engaged in.

Over time, you will develop more mindfulness regarding your thoughts, feelings, and habits. You will also have a visual representation of your progress. Use this weekly log to track your thoughts and habits.

Example: *Monday: I am working hard today; I feel proud of my efforts; I checked my calendar to stay on top of my commitments.*

DAY OF THE WEEK	POSITIVE THOUGHT	POSITIVE EMOTION	HEALTHY HABIT
MONDAY			
TUESDAY			
WEDNESDAY			
THURSDAY			
FRIDAY			
SATURDAY			
SUNDAY			

21 DAYS OF UNDOING A BAD HABIT

Consistency is key to not only building new habits but also to eliminating unwanted bad habits. Tracking how often you don't engage in a habit helps provide a visual representation of your progress.

Use this exercise as a twenty-one-day challenge. Pick a bad habit you want to eliminate. Track each day you do not engage in that habit for the next twenty-one days by crossing off each day. At the end of the twenty-one days, take time to briefly reflect on your progress. How do you feel about your efforts to eliminate this habit? What changes have you noticed in your behaviors? What can you improve on in the future?

Habit I am breaking: _____

Start Date: _____

End Date: _____

1	2	3	4	5	6	7
8	9	10	11	12	13	14
15	16	17	18	19	20	21

DAILY HEALTHY HABIT LOG

An easy way to ensure you're regularly engaging in healthy habits, and that the habits are having a positive impact, is by creating a daily healthy habit log. Scheduling your habits helps you get them done. Write down one healthy habit per day that you will complete. These can be any of the healthy habits you identified in previous chapters. Then, note any emotions you have after completing the healthy habit.

Example: *Monday: Stretched for 15 mins; 6:00 pm; Calm and relaxed.*

DAY OF THE WEEK	HEALTHY HABIT	TIME	EMOTIONS AFTER ACTIVITY
MONDAY			
TUESDAY			
WEDNESDAY			
THURSDAY			
FRIDAY			
SATURDAY			
SUNDAY			

Key Takeaways

■ Your thoughts influence your emotions and behaviors. This is known as the cognitive triangle.

■ Practicing mindfulness can help you become more aware of your automatic responses to situations.

■ Your thoughts are not always objective and true so it's important to question negative thoughts.

■ You can replace automatic negative thoughts with positive ones, which will positively change your emotions and behaviors.

CHAPTER 6

Follow the ABCs of Behavior Modification

Now that you are clear on CBT techniques, it's time to practice the evidence-based strategies of Behavior Modification. Behavior Modification is similar to CBT because it can help you create positive habits, but this technique focuses less on changing negative thoughts and more on the behavior loop (see page 6).

Throughout this chapter, you will learn ways to track and modify cues and consequences. You will also gain a deeper understanding of how long-term and short-term consequences affect your goals. Additionally, you will identify how to implement these new prompts into your daily life. If necessary, feel free to modify prompts to fit your unique needs. Consistency is more valuable than perfection.

David Mends a Bad Habit

David wanted to eliminate a bad habit he had recently acquired–
skipping his morning workout class. David had begun snoozing his
alarm and sleeping through his scheduled class. He used to be able to
get up, turn off his alarm, and get dressed for the workout class with
more ease. He acknowledged that the immediate feeling of sleeping
in helped him get more rest, but in the long term, it interfered with
his movement goals. David was confused and frustrated.

Then one day, David gave himself time and space to mindfully
reflect on what had prompted the change in his habit. David exam-
ined his environment and realized that he recently moved the
location where he kept his alarm clock. In the past David had placed
his alarm clock across the room, but he had recently moved it to the
nightstand within arm's reach. He thought this would make getting
up in the morning more convenient. David recognized that when
he used to get out of bed to turn off his alarm, it helped wake him
up, and he would immediately get in the habit of putting on his gym
clothes. Changing that one prompt in his environment changed the
entire habit chain.

David returned his alarm clock to its previous position across
the room from his bed. He was then able to let go of his bad habit
and reengage with his good habit. After seven days of waking up
on time and not sleeping in, he celebrated by scheduling time for a
restorative nap.

EACH DAY I MOVE CLOSER TO MY GOALS THROUGH THE HEALTHY HABITS I BUILD.

Think of a negative habit you would like to replace. What are the short-term rewards of doing this habit (e.g., stress relief, relaxation, entertainment)? How do those rewards make you feel?

_____

_____

_____

_____

_____

_____

Keep in mind the negative habit you identified in the previous prompt. What are the long-term consequences of you doing this habit (e.g., less time to do other things, poor health)? How do those consequences make you feel?

_____

_____

_____

_____

_____

_____

Antecedent Awareness

Antecedents are events, actions, thoughts, or circumstances that happen immediately before a behavior or habit. For example, putting on your pajamas may be the antecedent to brushing your teeth.

Strengthen your awareness of the various antecedents in your daily life to see what is prompting you to engage in habits, both good and bad. A stronger awareness of the antecedents impacting your habits gives you insights on how to change or strengthen them.

Start by looking at the habits you already do daily, such as brushing your teeth, getting into bed, eating lunch, etc. When you are about to engage in one of those habits, take a mindful moment to slow down the process. Take note of what triggered you to start that habit. Write down the various antecedents in your life. See if you notice any patterns or useful information that can aid you as you build and strengthen antecedents moving forward. You do not need to alter any antecedents you notice; for this practice, you should just focus on building your awareness.

IDENTIFY PROMPTS AND REWARDS OF A BAD HABIT

In order to eliminate a bad habit, you need to understand what prompts you to do that habit as well as the immediate reward you get from it.

For this exercise, you will select three bad habits you want to change. Pay attention to these habits over the next seven days. Then log what you've identified as the prompt and the reward for each habit. Afterward, consider the following questions to help you develop further insights: How can you alter these prompts so that you don't engage in the bad habit to begin with? What good habits would help you receive the same rewards as the bad habits?

HABIT	PROMPT	REWARD
Staying up late watching TV	Finishing dinner and turning on TV	Relaxing in front of TV after a stressful day

Think of a positive habit you are implementing. What are some ways you can make the short-term consequences of this habit more immediately satisfying (e.g., checking it off a list, having a celebration, taking a short break)? List as many ideas as you can without censoring yourself. Simply let the ideas flow.

Keep in mind the positive habit you reflected on in the previous question. What are the long-term benefits you get from this habit (e.g., increasing physical strength, having more time to spend with family, completing a creative project)? List as many positive consequences as you can. Recognizing the long-term benefits of a healthy habit can help you stay motivated in the present.

CREATE PROMPTS AND REWARDS FOR A GOOD HABIT

To help you successfully create a new healthy habit, you can consciously select the prompt that precedes the habit and the reward that follows and reinforces it. For this exercise, select three healthy habits you would like to implement into your daily life. Then select the prompt and reward for each habit. To make sure the prompts and rewards fit each habit, keep in mind factors, such as time of day, environment, and other people that may be around you. Make the prompts as easy as possible, and make the rewards as immediate and enjoyable as possible.

HABIT	PROMPT	REWARD
Drinking water	*Checking a text message*	*Feeling hydrated and tracking each cup of water I drink to see my progress for the day*

Mindfully Brush Your Teeth

Mindfulness is about being fully aware and engaged in the present moment. You can enhance mindfulness through each stage of the behavior loop (antecedent, behavior, consequence). For this practice, you will focus on mindfully engaging in a mundane task: brushing your teeth!

The next time you brush your teeth, do the following practice. Prior to brushing your teeth, notice what time of day it is. Notice what activity you do right beforehand. How are you feeling? What thoughts come to mind? When brushing your teeth, direct your attention to the sensation of the bristles on your gums, teeth, and tongue. Notice the smell of the toothpaste. Focus on any tastes. What is your speed? Where do you start in your mouth and where do you finish brushing? Allow yourself to be completely absorbed in the activity. Keep yourself in the present moment. What sensations do you notice after?

Your Environments as Antecedents

Certain environments, or changes in your environment, can act as antecedents. For example, walking into your kitchen may cue you to look for a snack. Being in a library can inhibit distractions such as talking. Environments influence your habits by either reinforcing them or inhibiting them.

For this practice, the aim is to increase mindful awareness of how a single environment influences your thoughts, emotions, and behaviors.

1. Begin by selecting one environment you inhabit on a regular basis, such as your home, work, vehicle, school, etc.

2. The next time you are in this environment, consider the following questions to increase your awareness:

    *   What emotions do you feel in this space?

    *   What thoughts do you associate with this environment?

    *   What habits do you engage in here?

    *   Does this environment invoke your healthy habits or inhibit them?

    *   Are there any changes you can realistically make to this environment so that it prompts healthy habits?

You can use this practice in different environments you frequent to help you consciously create antecedents to support your healthy habits and goals.

How Do You Celebrate?

One key element in the behavior loop is the consequence of a behavior or habit. The consequence can either repel you from wanting to repeat a habit or reinforce that habit so that you keep doing it. You can also reframe consequences as rewards for when you do good new habits. Rewards will help you develop positive associations with the habit you're trying to build. It's likely you already do this in your life without realizing it. For example, you can celebrate completing a habit by saying a positive statement out loud or to yourself like, "I am doing an awesome job today." Or you can reward yourself with a five-minute break. Rewards can take many forms as long as they make you feel good and reinforce the habit.

For this practice, use the next seven days to build awareness around the rewards you use for yourself. Reflect on the following questions at the end of each day:

- How do you celebrate your good habits?

- What do those rewards look like?

- How do you feel after a reward?

- Have you tried any rewards that did not work for you? Why?

- Are there habits you're struggling to stick with where a reward would be helpful?

You do not need to alter anything at this time. The aim of this practice is to strengthen your awareness. Approach these reflections with openness and curiosity to help you learn more about yourself.

Consciously Examine Consequences

Providing yourself the mental space to understand the long-term consequences of a bad habit is a great initial step toward creating the changes you want.

For this practice, you will engage in a mindful reflection to help you consciously examine those consequences. Keep a mindset of curiosity and non-judgment. The goal is to help you consciously understand the long-term consequences of a habit to inform your present-day decisions. It may be helpful to find a quiet and comfortable space to sit and reflect.

To begin, select a negative habit that you know provides you with an immediate reward. Once you've identified the habit, take time to mindfully reflect on the following:

- If you continue this habit, how will it impact you over the next year?

- If you continue this habit, what will your life look like as a result in 10 years?

- What are some negative thoughts, emotions, and other behaviors that may come from this habit over time?

- How might your life look different if you were to eliminate this habit?

- Imagine that you decided to change this habit for the better. What would help you do it?

- Who could offer support in making this change?

One New Prompt

Now that you have begun to develop your awareness of the prompts, habits, and consequences in your daily life, you can take this self-awareness one step further. For this practice, you will identify one potential prompt that you can use to cue a good habit.

Take note of things you do routinely and daily. Maybe these are behaviors you typically do without thinking, but you can bring attention to them now. Some examples include checking your phone, making your bed, and washing your hands. Be mindful of any thoughts and feelings that come up when you're doing these activities to assess if they would be good prompts for healthy habits.

Once you've identified your new prompt, select the good habit that will go with it. Practice doing the habit immediately after you do the prompt. For example, if the habit you are trying to build is drinking more water, you can use checking your cell phone as a prompt. You could make an agreement with yourself that, "Every time I check my cell phone, I will take a sip of water."

Practice this new prompt and habit combination as often as you like. Treat this practice as an experiment to see if this new prompt is an effective way to engage in your selected habit. Notice any wins or challenges you encounter. Make mindful alterations to this prompt as needed.

LEVERAGE OLD HABITS

An effective strategy for creating new habits is to leverage old ones. You can use old habits as antecedents for new ones. Some examples of old habits you may already have in place that could function as antecedents include making your morning cup of coffee, changing into your pajamas, taking your vitamins, and making your bed in the morning. The key is to pair your habits by immediately doing the new habit after the old.

Example: *After I make my morning cup of coffee, I will write down one thing I am grateful for.*

For this exercise, you will identify five old habits you will leverage as antecedents to build new habits.

1. After I (old habit) _____ ,

   I will (new habit) _____ .

2. After I (old habit) _____ ,

   I will (new habit) _____ .

3. After I (old habit) _____ ,

   I will (new habit) _____ .

4. After I (old habit) _____ ,

   I will (new habit) _____ .

5. After I (old habit) _____ ,

   I will (new habit) _____ .

IDENTIFY THE RIGHT ANTECEDENT

As you've seen, antecedents are a key part of habit change, as they cue your desired habit. Think of antecedents as the foundation of habit change. Antecedents can be especially helpful if they occur naturally and/or daily.

In this exercise, you will go through the list of suggested antecedents and check off the ones that are right for you and your habits. You can also write down additional ideas for antecedents that may pertain to your life specifically.

Ideas for Antecedents:

☐ Sunrise

☐ Getting out of bed in the morning

☐ Brushing your teeth

☐ Eating breakfast

☐ Getting dressed for the day

☐ Making a morning cup of coffee

☐ Driving to work

☐ Washing your hands

☐ Eating lunch

☐ Sunset

☐ Getting a text message

☐ Getting an email message

☐ Turning off your computer

☐ Eating dinner

☐ Changing into pajamas

☐ Getting into bed

☐ _____

☐ _____

☐ _____

TRACK YOUR HABIT LOOPS

The habit loop consists of ABC: Antecedent (A) → Behavior (B) → Consequence (C). Tracking each step in the loop will help ingrain it into your routine.

For this exercise, you will select one habit and track the process by marking off the table below as you complete each element of the loop for twenty-one days.

Habit:

Antecedent (A)

Behavior (B)

Consequence (C)

	1	2	3	4	5	6	7	8	9	10	11	12	13	14	15	16	17	18	19	20	21
A																					
B																					
C																					

IDEAS FOR HEALTHY CELEBRATIONS

Celebrations are a great tool to reinforce a good habit. However, you want to be sure the celebration keeps you in alignment with your goals and values. The celebration shouldn't interfere with the overall goal. For example, if your goal is to reduce your sugar intake, you would not want to celebrate a week without excess sugar by eating a frosted cupcake. Celebrations don't have to be big, but they should be satisfying, and they should align with your goal.

In this exercise, you will see a list of suggested healthy celebrations. Check off the celebrations you'd like to implement and add additional ideas at the end of the list. Remember, these suggested celebrations can be modified to fit your needs, goals, and values.

Suggested Healthy Celebrations:

☐ Start a new journal

☐ Have a game night with friends

☐ Watch the sunrise or sunset

☐ Try a new hobby

☐ Play your favorite childhood game

☐ Spend time in nature

☐ Read a book

☐ Listen to happy music

☐ Share your accomplishment with someone else

☐ Take a day off to relax

☐ Watch a funny movie

☐ Try a new workout class

☐ Make your favorite cup of tea

☐ Have dinner with a loved one

☐ Get a massage

☐ _____

☐ _____

☐ _____

CREATE WEEKLY CELEBRATIONS

Consistency with your positive habits is key to reaching your goals. Weekly celebrations can help you remain consistent and motivated. This exercise will help you plan out and track celebrations.

Select one positive habit you're committing to doing consistently, every day, for one week. Each day, circle whether you participated in the habit. If you select "No" for the day, practice self-compassion as you reflect on what obstacles may have gotten in your way. At the end of the week, have a small celebration for your consistency.

After seven days of _____ ,

I will reward myself by _____ .

DAY	HABIT COMPLETED
1	Yes / No
2	Yes / No
3	Yes / No
4	Yes / No
5	Yes / No
6	Yes / No
7	Yes / No

Key Takeaways

- Mindful awareness of the habit loop, Antecedent ➜ Behavior ➜ Consequence, can provide you with insights on how to change and create habits.

- Antecedents can be people, places, times of day, or even habits that you've already established.

- It is important to consider both the short-term and long-term consequences of a habit.

- Celebrations that keep you aligned with your goals are a great tool to reinforce a good habit.

CHAPTER 7

Manage Urges, Triggers, and Self-Sabotage

I f you've ever succumbed to temptations or snapped back into unwanted habits, you're not alone. Sustainable habit change is not a matter of willpower. There are real obstacles that can make it harder to maintain good habits no matter how badly you may want to. The key to overcoming these obstacles is having the right information and tools. This chapter will focus on identifying triggers that can get in the way of your positive habits and goals.

For the purposes of this book, think of triggers as cues that can bring you back into unhealthy habits. An urge is an impulse, usually sudden, to engage in a behavior. In this chapter, you will find tools for managing urges and addressing root causes of self-sabotaging behaviors. Among the tools are prompts, practices, and exercises designed to support you. You've already done great work throughout this book; use this chapter to help you maintain positive changes.

Sebastian Beats the Urge

For as long as he could remember, Sebastian had been biting his nails. Sebastian unsuccessfully tried to quit this habit several times and had given up his efforts, until his doctor explained that nail biting was having negative consequences on his health. That is when Sebastian recognized that he had to eliminate this habit once and for all.

Sebastian's doctor recommended that he pay attention to what triggered his nail biting and note when urges to bite his nails arose. Sebastian decided to track his nail-biting habit to recognize any triggers. After about a week of consistent tracking, Sebastian noticed that stress was a trigger to his nail-biting, such as when he was stuck in traffic or about to give a presentation at work. Once he knew the cause of the unhealthy habit, he could identify a positive habit to replace it with.

After some research, Sebastian learned about the tool of urge surfing (see page 124). He used this mindfulness technique every time he noticed the trigger of stress and felt the urge to bite his nails. Urge surfing helped him move past the urge to bite his nails. Over time this helped him reduce stress and identify other positive coping strategies in lieu of nail biting. This unhealthy habit of biting his nails when stressed was no longer an urge that Sebastian had to manage.

> I AM PROUD OF HOW FAR I'VE COME,
> AND I WILL CONTINUE WORKING TOWARD
> A HAPPY AND HEALTHY LIFE.

Reflect on the times you've struggled to maintain healthy habits. What behaviors did you notice contributed to your struggles?

_____

_____

_____

_____

_____

_____

Ask yourself: If I think about the good habits I'm implementing, what are some obstacles that may get in the way of remaining consistent?

_____

_____

_____

_____

_____

_____

KNOW YOUR TENDENCIES QUIZ

Utilize this quiz to get a clear understanding of how urges, triggers, and self-sabotaging behaviors may affect your healthy habit goals. After each statement, circle the number that most applies to you:

0 = Never, 1 = Rarely, 2 = Sometimes, 3 = Often, 4 = Almost Always, 5 = Always

I find it easy to manage urges that lead to unhealthy habits.

0   1   2   3   4   5

It's not very challenging for me to recognize triggers.

0   1   2   3   4   5

I am able to recognize my self-sabotaging behaviors.

0   1   2   3   4   5

When urges, triggers, and self-sabotaging temptations arise, I am able to ask others for help.

0   1   2   3   4   5

I have concrete strategies to help cope with urges and triggers.

0   1   2   3   4   5

I know how to make unhealthy habits inconvenient and, therefore, less tempting.

0   1   2   3   4   5

I regularly reflect on my self-sabotaging behaviors to learn from my past.

0   1   2   3   4   5

If I fall back into old unhealthy habits, I am not too hard on myself.

0   1   2   3   4   5

I rely on mindfulness techniques to help manage difficult emotions.

0   1   2   3   4   5

I am aware how different environments impact my ability to stick with healthy habits.

0   1   2   3   4   5

Scoring: Review your responses to the above statements. Take notice of the areas where you scored highly (4 to 5) and which scores were low (0 to 2). Do you notice any patterns? How can these results inform your habit strategies moving forward?

Bad Habit Trigger Awareness

The first step in mitigating triggers for unhealthy habits is to recognize them. A trigger can be anything that cues unhealthy habits you once had. Some examples of triggers include a specific place, something someone says to you, or another habit. It is common to react to triggers subconsciously, so raising your awareness around them can empower you to choose differently.

  The objective of this exercise is to simply raise awareness without judgment. You will not be taking any additional actions aside from increasing your awareness. To raise awareness of potential triggers for an unhealthy habit you are trying to eliminate, engage in the following steps:

1. Begin by selecting one unhealthy habit you would like to release. Once you've identified the habit, close your eyes, if you're in a secure space to do so.

2. Take three long, deep breaths in. Allow your mind and body to sink into this moment.

3. Using your available senses, visualize yourself engaging in this unhealthy habit.

4. Allow your mind to float back in time to right before you initiated this unhealthy habit. What were you doing then? What senses or emotions did you notice?

5. Float back in time even further, taking note of your surroundings, thoughts, and actions. Continue until you've landed on the trigger that set this unhealthy habit into motion.

6. Once you've landed on the trigger, do not judge yourself. Instead, allow yourself to curiously observe this trigger.

7. After you've gleaned all of the information that you feel is valuable, take three more long, deep breaths. Whenever you are ready, you may open your eyes if they are closed.

TAKE A CLOSER LOOK AT YOUR TEMPTATIONS

Temptations to give into unhealthy urges and restart bad habits are a common experience. Understanding temptations can help you be free of them.

To understand the causes, consequences, and potential solutions for your temptations, you can respond to the following prompts:

The last time you felt tempted to engage in an unhealthy habit was:

How did you feel after you gave into that temptation?

In the future, instead of giving into this temptation, what would you rather do?

Some examples of times you've been able to manage temptations include:

Question Your Triggers with Curiosity

Once you've identified an unhealthy habit you would like to change, and raised your awareness of the trigger(s) for that habit, you may be ready to reflect further.

Keep a mindset of curiosity as you take time to reflect on the following questions. If you find it helpful, you can also discuss these questions with a trusted friend or loved one.

- What happened during the trigger?

- What emotions came up for you?

- Have you been in a similar situation before? Did you react in the same way?

- How would you prefer to react?

After you've given yourself time to curiously reflect on each question, you can use your answers to inform how you would prefer to cope with triggers in the future.

TRACK UNHEALTHY URGES

A key way to gain a better understanding of urges that you've evaluated as unhealthy is to track them.

Write down any unhealthy urges that come up for you each day. Log whether or not you follow through on the urge, and how you feel afterward.

DAY OF THE WEEK	UNHEALTHY URGE	FOLLOWED THROUGH ON URGE? (YES/NO)	EMOTIONS AFTER
Monday	Urge to skip my workout for the day	No	Proud and energized
MONDAY			
TUESDAY			
WEDNESDAY			
THURSDAY			
FRIDAY			
SATURDAY			
SUNDAY			

Urge Surf to Manage Temptations

Urge surfing is a technique you can utilize to observe and experience your feelings without giving into the temptation of acting on your urge. You can think of experiencing an urge like a wave in the ocean. Imagine yourself as a surfer riding the wave of an urge. Even the strongest ocean waves will pass; similarly, your urges can feel intense, but in reality do not last long.

To practice urge surfing the next time an urge arises, use the following steps:

1. Connect with your breath by paying attention to how you are breathing. You do not need to control your breath at this point. Simply follow your normal breath from the beginning of an in-breath all the way through the end of an out-breath. Pay attention to how the air feels entering your body. Be mindful of any rising and falling in your chest or stomach. Stay connected to your breath cycles for as long as you need.

2. Notice if your thoughts have started to wander. If so, that's okay. Gently pull your thoughts back into the presence of your breath. It's completely normal for your mind to wander, and even be brought back to the temptation. Each time your thoughts begin to wander, just bring them back to the breath.

3. Visualize your urge to engage in a temptation reaching its peak and losing its force the way that a wave does as it crumbles onto the shore. Continue to visualize this image and breathe for as long as you need.

4. Once you feel that the temptation to engage in an urge has passed, move on from this practice by doing something restorative for yourself, such as a gentle stretch or drinking a glass of water.

Make Unhealthy Urges Inconvenient

If it's extremely challenging for you to resist an unhealthy urge, then it's important for you to implement a strategy of inconvenience. Essentially, your aim is to make engaging in this unhealthy urge as inconvenient as possible. You are much less likely to give into this urge if it's not convenient for you to do so.

Take time to reflect on and potentially implement the following strategies to make unhealthy urges inconvenient:

• Can you create space between yourself and an unhealthy urge?

  Example: *You need to get work done, but keep giving into the urge of checking your phone. Create space by leaving your phone in a different room.*

• Is there someone who can act as a barrier between you and this urge?

  Example: *You are trying to reduce your sugar intake, but there's always candy at your workplace. You can ask a coworker to keep the candy in their office so that each time you want to get a piece you have to knock on their door and ask them.*

• Out of sight, out of mind! Can you keep your unhealthy urge out of sight?

  Example: *Your goal is to shop less and save more, but every day on your drive home, you pass the same boutique and often give in to the urge to stop and shop. To keep this boutique out of sight and out of mind, you can take an alternate route home.*

RESPOND TO NEGATIVE TRIGGERS WITH POSITIVE RESPONSES

You can counteract negative triggers by replacing them with positive responses.

In this exercise, you will identify negative triggers, how you typically respond, and new positive responses. Having the trigger and positive response both clearly identified will prepare you to respond in a healthy way the next time you encounter that trigger. Use the following format to fill in the blanks.

Example:

A negative trigger for you is *hearing gossip.*

You typically respond by *joining in on the gossip.*

The next time this trigger comes up you will *change the subject instead.*

A negative trigger for you is _____

_____

_____ .

You typically respond by _____

_____

_____ .

The next time this trigger comes up you will _____

_____

_____ .

A negative trigger for you is

                                                                   .

You typically respond by

                                                                    .

The next time this trigger comes up you will

                                                                    .

A negative trigger for you is

                                                                    .

You typically respond by

                                                                    .

The next time this trigger comes up you will

                                                                    .

Understand Why You Self-Sabotage

It is common to engage in self-sabotaging habits for a variety of reasons. Understanding the reasons behind self-sabotage can help you prevent it in the future.

Create time and space to mindfully reflect on questions regarding your own self-sabotaging tendencies. If you find it helpful, you can also discuss these questions with a trusted friend or family member. Keep an open and curious mind as you reflect on the following questions:

- What is an example of a self-sabotaging behavior you've done in the past?

- How did you feel after self-sabotaging?

- Where in your body did you notice these feelings?

- Does this behavior align with your values and goals?

- How can you be more mindful of self-sabotage in the future?

COMMON WAYS TO SELF-SABOTAGE

Self-sabotaging often happens unconsciously, without you even realizing it. In order to identify how you may be prone to unconsciously self-sabotaging your own success, it's crucial that you raise awareness around your own tendencies.

Utilize the following list to review some of the most common ways people self-sabotage. Check off any methods that resonate with your experiences. Feel free to write down any additional behaviors you think of in the space provided.

☐ **Procrastination:** putting things off until the last possible minute and causing stress

☐ **Emphasizing the negatives:** highlighting and focusing on only the negatives of a situation

☐ **Overthinking:** thinking about things so much it causes stress and inhibits action

☐ **Assuming:** holding yourself back because you assume the worst will always happen

☐ **Downplaying successes:** not acknowledging your progress or celebrating your wins

☐ **Controlling:** insisting that you have control over everything instead of asking for support

☐ **Black-and-white thinking:** believing that you either have to do things perfectly or not at all

☐ _____

Box Breathing to Manage Urges, Triggers, and Self-Sabotaging

A simple strategy to resist urges, triggers, temptations, and self-sabotaging habits is to engage in a simple mindfulness practice. A manageable technique to help ground you and move past unhealthy behaviors is called "box breathing." This technique helps reduce stress and increase mindfulness.

To engage in box breathing to manage habit challenges, follow these steps:

1. Relax your body. You can sit, stand, or lie down.

2. Observe your natural breath for about one minute.

3. Next, if it's comfortable to do so, place one hand on your stomach and continue to connect with your breath.

4. Breathe in slowly while counting to four. Notice the air rising in your stomach.

5. Hold your breath while counting to four.

6. Slowly exhale your breath while counting to four. Notice the air being released.

7. Repeat steps 3 through 6 until you feel grounded.

Do you have any urges that can get in the way of your goals? What are these urges and how often do they show up in your life?

What techniques do you already have that help you manage unhealthy urges? How can you use these techniques during your current habit change journey?

REFLECT FOR SUCCESS

It's important to plan for successful management of urges, triggers, and self-sabotaging behaviors. Planning ahead gives you a better chance of successfully sticking to your healthy habits and achieving your goals.

Consider the different situations in the statements below and describe how you might handle them.

Some examples of how you typically handle urges, triggers, and self-sabotaging behaviors include:

Some signs that triggers are impacting your behavior include:

The next time an unhealthy urge arises, what can you do to cope?

When you notice yourself engaging in self-sabotaging behaviors, how will you get support in the future?

If stress or overwhelm are tempting you to go back to unhealthy habits, what mindfulness techniques can you use to manage your emotions?

WRITE YOUR OWN AFFIRMATIONS

Affirmations are powerful mindset tools. In this exercise, you will use a simple formula to create your own affirmations that will help you manage urges, triggers, and self-sabotaging behaviors, and also motivate you to continue with healthy habits.

Use the following steps to create your affirmations:

1. Start with "I," "I am," or "My" to ensure each statement is focused on empowering you.

2. Write your affirmations in the present tense.

3. Keep each statement positive.

4. Use emotions to make your affirmations powerful.

5. Keep affirmations brief so that they're easy for you to remember and repeat when needed.

Examples: *I am creating a life that brings me joy and peace; My healthy habits bring me closer to my dreams; I am joyfully celebrating my habit successes.*

Affirmations:

Key Takeaways

- Urges, triggers, and self-sabotaging behaviors are normal and do not reflect a lack of willpower.

- Mindfulness strategies, such as urge surfing, can help you manage urges, triggers, and unhealthy habits.

- Awareness is key to mitigating and changing urges, temptations, and self-sabotage.

- You can build awareness through reflection, self check-ins, and tracking your behaviors.

CHAPTER 8

Monitor Your Habits to Sustain Success

So far, you've deepened your understanding of habits, identified your goals, learned the proven techniques of habit change, and even gained an understanding of how to prevent falling back into unhealthy habits. Congratulations! You've done excellent work so far! Next, you will harness the skills needed to maintain the good habits you are forming. Throughout this chapter you will learn how to remain mindful of your habits and properly monitor them so that you can continue on the positive path of reaching your goals. This chapter will support you in maintaining all of your new and improved habits—not just for today, but for the long-term as well.

Fiona Finds Her Habit Strategies

Fiona was a college senior just a few months from graduating when she realized she felt stuck with the prospect of so many decisions to make. Where should she live? What type of job should she get? Should she consider graduate school? Fiona was worried she would not achieve success.

She discussed these concerns with her guidance counselor, who asked Fiona, "What do *you* define as success?" Fiona was speechless. She realized she didn't know the answer to this important question. That is when Fiona's guidance counselor suggested she practice mindfulness to help reduce her anxiety and build her self-awareness. Fiona had never tried any mindfulness techniques before, but she was open to starting.

By the time graduation came, Fiona had learned a variety of mindfulness techniques to help her reduce stress and better understand her thoughts, emotions, and behaviors. She had a calmer and clearer perspective on life after graduation. However, her mindfulness practices did not end there.

Years later, Fiona remains consistent with practicing mindfulness to help her monitor her habits. Her monitoring techniques and mindfulness practices have changed and evolved along with other aspects of Fiona's life, but she's continuously completed and tracked her habits in fun and accessible ways. Fiona now has a toolbox full of methods to manage feelings of anxiety and stress, and she's able to regularly observe her emotions, thoughts, and behaviors. Fiona remains grateful to have started mindfulness practices years ago.

I AM CAPABLE OF ACHIEVING MY GOALS AND EMBODYING A LIFE THAT I LOVE.

Reflect back on all the work you've done. What successes have you noticed in your habit change journey so far? How can you celebrate these successes?

Consider the work you've done in previous chapters. What have you learned about yourself? What have you learned about creating and eliminating habits?

HABIT PROGRESS QUIZ

Take a closer look at how your habits have changed as you've implemented new techniques. This quiz will help you evaluate progress and areas for growth related to your habits and overall goals. After each statement, circle the number that most applies to you.

0 = Strongly Disagree, 1 = Disagree, 2 = Undecided, 3 = Somewhat Agree, 4 = Agree, 5 = Strongly Agree

I have identified effective ways to track my habits.

0   1   2   3   4   5

It's clear to me how my habits impact my goals.

0   1   2   3   4   5

When setting new goals, I always use the S.M.A.R.T. goals method.

0   1   2   3   4   5

I make time to celebrate my successes.

0   1   2   3   4   5

I have identified people in my life who support my healthy habits.

0   1   2   3   4   5

Engaging in mindfulness has become a part of my habit change strategy.

0   1   2   3   4   5

I have made adjustments to my environment(s) to support positive habits and reduce negative ones.

0   1   2   3   4   5

Even when I struggle to maintain healthy habits, I am compassionate with myself.

0   1   2   3   4   5

I have identified coping strategies to help manage negative temptations.

0   1   2   3   4   5

I no longer believe that successful habit change is solely based on willpower.

0   1   2   3   4   5

I have a clearer understanding of how my thoughts, feelings, and behaviors affect each other.

0   1   2   3   4   5

Scoring: Review your responses to the above statements. Take notice of the areas where you scored highly (4 to 5) and which scores were low (0 to 2). Do you notice any patterns? Are there areas you would like to continue improving? Are there areas where you've made progress?

Reconnect with Your Goals

To help maintain motivation and consistency for positive habit change, you can use this practice to reconnect with the goals you identified in chapter 3.

Use the following steps to center your thoughts and awareness and reflect:

1. Find a comfortable place to sit or lie down. Ground yourself by taking three long, deep breaths.

2. Release any tension you may be carrying. Relax your shoulders, unclench your jaw, and make any additional adjustments needed to relax your body as much as possible.

3. Connect with your breath and how it moves through your body. If at any point during this mindful reflection you begin to feel distracted or agitated, come back to your breath.

4. Reflect on one specific goal at a time as you consider the following:

   - What do you find exciting about this goal?

   - What do you find challenging about this goal?

   - Does this goal continue to align with your values?

   - When you visualize your future self that has achieved this goal, how do you feel?

   - What habits did you create or let go of to help you get to achieve this goal?

FOCUS Technique for Mindful Awareness

It can be challenging to maintain mindful awareness as you work toward your long-term goals. It's especially difficult when you face setbacks on your habit-change journey. However, setbacks can be seen as feedback, guiding you to improve and make changes if necessary.

You can use the FOCUS Technique to help you get clear on the feedback you've received and remain focused on your long-term goal. Follow these steps to engage in this mindful awareness practice:

Feel: Start by feeling in the present moment. Notice where your body is connecting with the ground. Feel your breath flowing in and out of your lungs. Feel the concrete things around you to help your body and mind get grounded.

Observe: Take time to observe feelings you are having about this setback. Do not try to judge or alter these feelings. Are you angry? Frustrated? Disappointed? Are you experiencing indifference or confusion? Whatever is coming up for you now, observe it.

Curious: Be curious about these feelings. What are they trying to tell you? What can you learn about yourself from these feelings?

Understand: Use this information to understand what is important to you. Understand if this habit still aligns with your goal, or if this goal still aligns with your values. Understand if there are any adjustments that you can make.

Stop: Stop before you take action to get clear on the thoughts, feelings, and potential conclusions you identified in the previous steps. Stop before you act to make sure your next action is aligned with your overall goals and values.

TRACK YOUR HABITS LONG-TERM

You may need a little more accountability and support as you continue to work on your habits for the long-term. That's perfectly normal and doable. You can positively reinforce the small steps you're taking by tracking your positive habits throughout each month.

Use the chart below to keep track of five habits over a month-long period of time. At the top, write in the month. On each blank line, fill in the habit you will track. Then, find fun and creative ways to track whether or not a habit was completed. Use any method that sounds sustainable for you.

MONTH:

DAILY HABITS	1	2	3	4	5	6	7	8	9	10	11
Example: 8 hours of sleep											

12	13	14	15	16	17	18	19	20	21	22	23	24	25	26	27	28	29	30	31

Observe How a Habit Makes You Feel

To assess if you'd like to continue with a habit, you can use this mindfulness practice to better understand how a habit is making you feel.

This practice will help you identify any thoughts, feelings, and bodily sensations related to specific habits. Identify one habit at a time as you complete the following steps to increase your awareness.

1. Engage in the habit you'd like to assess.

2. Immediately after finishing this habit, take a few moments to pause.

3. What do you notice in your body? What thoughts come up? What feelings are present?

4. Do not change or alter anything at this phase. Simply take note of your thoughts, feelings, and potential responses in your body.

You may immediately notice positive or negative reactions, or it may take practice. Repeat this exercise with the same habit, if needed, or utilize it with a new habit.

When do you feel the least motivated to continue with your healthy habits? What strategies can you use to stay on track?

Know yourself better to ensure success. Everyone responds to cues differently. What are some creative ways to make monitoring your habits more satisfying?

Mindful Movement
for Reflection

If you would like to engage in a more active form of mindfulness to reflect on your habits and goals, then mindful movement is a great strategy. Mindful movements help increase awareness and provide space to reflect on habits.

Before you begin the mindful movement, identify a calm and quiet space to move. This space could be outdoors or indoors depending on what works best for you. The point is to take yourself off autopilot and be engaged. Use the following steps to embark on your mindful walk:

1. As you begin, move at a natural pace that feels comfortable to you. Notice your breath. Do you feel it in your stomach or chest? Is your breath quick or slow?

2. With each movement, notice your body. Notice each and every move you make. You do not need to judge any of your movements; simply build awareness.

3. Take time to notice your surroundings. Use all of your available senses to inventory your environment.

4. As you continue to move, take slow and deep breaths. Allow your body and movements to relax as much as possible.

5. Reflect on your habits and goals. What has worked well so far? What challenges have you faced? How can you continue to improve your habits moving forward? How are your thoughts and feelings impacting your habits lately?

Limit Distractions to Stay on Track

To ladder your habits toward bigger goals, it's important to remove distractions. The world can be full of distractions! Some inattentiveness is completely normal, but too many unnecessary distractions will prevent you from remaining aware of behaviors, thoughts, and feelings related to your habits.

Use this practice to take mindful inventory of different spaces where distractions are common. Take your time to review each space and make any distractions as inconvenient as possible, or remove them altogether, if possible.

- **Desk/workspace:** Is there any clutter that you could organize or tools you no longer need?

- **Phone/computer:** Are there any distraction-prone apps that you could hide or remove?

- **Bathroom:** Can you clear off any countertops or remove old toiletries that are taking up space?

- **Kitchen:** Are there any tempting treats that distract you from your health and wellness goals? Can you make these less appealing to reach for?

- **Main living space:** Do you easily get distracted by the TV or other forms of entertainment when you want to spend more time on your goals? Can you make it more challenging to reach for the remote to mitigate potential distractions?

HOW HABITS WILL IMPACT YOUR BIG GOALS

In this exercise you will be focusing your attention on how your current habit changes will impact the larger goals you've previously identified.

Consider and respond to the following questions as you reflect:

What are your three biggest goals right now?

Why will these goals help you live a happier and healthier life?

What does success in these goals look like?

How do your positive habits support your goals?

_____

_____

_____

_____

What are the tools and techniques that help you stay consistent with positive habits?

_____

_____

_____

_____

_____

What can you do when you need support in maintaining your healthy habits?

_____

_____

_____

_____

_____

CONTINUE MONITORING BAD HABITS

Monitoring is a powerful tool for building and eliminating habits. There are various methods you can use to monitor your abstinence from bad habits over the long term.

In this exercise, you will review a list of ideas and identify the ones you'd like to implement. You can also jot down any additional ideas you may have.

☐ Place money in a jar each time you engage in the bad habit.

☐ Use a stopwatch to time how long you do a bad habit.

☐ Tally the number of times you engage in the bad habit each day.

☐ Mark your calendar with a red "X" each day you engaged in the bad habit.

☐ Use a computer program to create a graph to track your bad habit.

☐ Pick an accountability buddy you can report to each time you do this bad habit.

☐ Keep a physical habit journal where you record whether you did the bad habit.

☐ Pick a small item to place in a glass container each time you do the bad habit (e.g., marbles in a fishbowl).

☐ Create your own visual bad-habit tracker where you can record whether or not you engaged in the bad habit each day.

☐ Find and use a free app on your phone to conveniently monitor your bad habit.

☐ _____

☐ _____

☐ _____

☐ _____

☐ _____

☐ _____

☐ _____

MINDFULNESS TECHNIQUES LOG

You have learned and rehearsed many mindfulness techniques to support your habit-change journey. These mindfulness techniques can be positive habits on their own.

Use this exercise to track your mindfulness habits. Note the date, time, and the mindfulness technique you used. Then, rate your mood prior to and after engaging in the mindfulness technique on a scale from 0 to 5, with 0 being very low mood and 5 being very positive mood.

DATE/TIME	MINDFULNESS TECHNIQUE	MOOD BEFORE (0 TO 5)	MOOD AFTER (0 TO 5)

CELEBRATORY REFLECTION

You've already made a lot of great progress on your habit-change journey. It's important to reflect on and celebrate successes to recognize your achievements as you continue working on positive habit change.

Consider the following as you reflect and support yourself in celebrating your growth and journey:

One big achievement you've noticed so far is:

Three small achievements you've noticed so far are:

What are some ways you can celebrate big successes?

What are some ways you can celebrate small successes?

Who are some people you can celebrate your successes with?

What are some methods you can use to track your successes?

CREATE YOUR IDEAL HABIT CALENDAR

Now that you've had the opportunity to identify, implement, and track your healthy habits, you can create your ideal habit calendar.

This twenty-one-day calendar has been left blank for you to fill in your own vision of ideally organized habits. Use this exercise as a fun and creative way to keep up with your habit goals.

MON	TUE	WED	THURS

FRI	SAT	SUN

Gratitude Meditation

A great way to continue with good habits is to be grateful for the effort you've put in and the progress you've already made. Developing a practice of gratitude can help you to remain consistent, even during challenging times.

   Use this gratitude meditation as often as you like to help you recognize your strength and continue with healthy habits.

1. Find a comfortable and quiet place to sit or lie down.

2. If it's comfortable, place one hand over your heart and begin to deepen your breath.

3. Ensure that your breathing feels easy, relaxed, and calming.

4. Pick one thing that you are grateful for on this journey of changing your habits and working toward your goals. Perhaps you are grateful for the support you've found in friends and family; perhaps you are grateful for your ability to keep trying; or perhaps you are grateful that your new habits are helping you to feel happier and healthier.

5. Whatever it is you are grateful for, no matter how big or small, focus on the positive feelings associated with this gratitude.

6. Imagine there is a warm light over your heart where you've placed your hand. Visualize how, as your gratitude deepens, this warm light grows bigger and bigger.

7. Continue to breathe in a relaxed manner and see if you can identify more things that you are grateful for. Notice how the light over your heart continues to expand.

8. Whenever you're ready, take three long and slow deep breaths as the feeling of gratitude washes over you.

9. Reflect back on this positive experience throughout your day, and use this meditation as often as you like.

Key Takeaways

- Monitoring habits and remaining mindful of goals will help you achieve long-term success.

- Use strategies to track long-term development of good habits as well as the avoidance of bad habits.

- Mindfulness practices will help you continue to stay aware of your emotions and actions.

- Reflection is a part of the process to help you ladder habits toward long-term goals.

A FINAL NOTE

Congratulations! You've made it through *The Better Habits Workbook*. Take a moment to acknowledge how far you've come in your habits journey. Now that you've learned the evidence-based information and put the tools into practice, I encourage you to continue keeping track of your habits and goals. Use the strategies and techniques that work best for you. You can always come back to review any of the techniques to help you continue to grow.

Additionally, I want to remind you to be self-compassionate. If you go back to old habits, do not engage in all-or-nothing thinking. Returning to a habit does not negate the amazing work you've done. Setbacks do not define you, and as you've witnessed, you are capable of creating positive change. I invite you to resume your positive practices and work toward your goals with the techniques you've learned. These strategies are always here for you.

Take time to reflect on and recognize your ability to learn and implement these habit strategies. Although this workbook provided you with the tools to make positive changes, you are the person who implemented these changes. Your efforts will continue to support your lifestyle, values, and goals moving forward. As you've seen throughout this journey, you really are capable of getting unstuck, changing your habits, and achieving your goals. You did it. Now it's time to celebrate!

RESOURCES

Books

Habits: A 12-Week Journal to Change Your Habits, Track Your Progress, and Achieve Your Goals by Dr. Hayden Finch

The Miracle of Mindfulness: An Introduction to the Practice of Meditation by Thich Nhat Hanh

Self-Compassion: The Proven Power of Being Kind to Yourself by Dr. Kristin Neff

Websites

NAMI.org/home: National Alliance on Mental Illness (disponible en español)

SAMHSA.gov: Substance Abuse and Mental Health Services Administration (disponible en español)

Podcasts

Happier with Gretchen Rubin: GretchenRubin.com/podcasts

Hidden Brain: HiddenBrain.org

REFERENCES

American Psychological Association. "What Is Cognitive Behavioral Therapy?" Practice Guideline for the Treatment of Posttraumatic Stress Disorder. July 2017. apa.org/ptsd-guideline/patients-and-families/cognitive-behavioral.

Andrew Jagim, P. D. "The Importance of Movement." Mayo Clinic Health System. June 5, 2020. mayoclinichealthsystem.org/hometown-health/featured-topic/the-importance-of-movement.

Asam—American Society of Addiction Medicine. American Society of Addiction Medicine (2022). Accessed January 18, 2022. asam.org/asam-criteria/about-the-asam-criteria.

Beck Institute. "Introduction to CBT." 2018. beckinstitute.org/about/understanding-cbt.

Beck, Judith S. *Cognitive Behavior Therapy: Basics and Beyond*. Guilford Press, 2011.

Hofmann, Stefan G., Anu Asnaani, Imke J. J. Vonk, Alice T. Sawyer, and Angela Fang. "The Efficacy of Cognitive Behavioral Therapy: A Review of Meta-Analyses." *Cognitive Therapy and Research* 36, no. 5 (2012): 427–40. doi.org/10.1007/s10608-012-9476-1.

Ivtzan, Itai, Tarli Young, Janis Martman, Allison Jeffery, Tim Lomas, Rona Hart, and Francisco Jose Eiroa-Orosa. "Integrating Mindfulness into Positive Psychology: A Randomised Controlled Trial of an Online Positive Mindfulness Program." *Mindfulness* 7 (July 2016), 1396–1407. doi.org/10.1007/s12671-016-0581-1.

Miltenberger, Raymond G. *Behavior Modification: Principles and Procedures*. Cengage Learning, 2015.

Scott, Hannah K., Ankit Jain, and Mark Cogburn. "Behavior Modification." StatPearls Publishing, November 2021. pubmed.ncbi.nlm.nih.gov/29083709.

INDEX

Habit Changing (*continued*)
  trigger awareness and, 122
  which habits to change, deciding on, 11
  willpower not sole factor in, 8, 12, 23, 59, 115
Habit Monitoring, 24, 54, 109, 137
  Daily Healthy Habit Log, 92
  in Goals and Habits Inventory Quiz, 32-33
  habit calendar, creating, 156
  Habits and Stress tracking form, 65
  Habits Throughout the Day tracking sheet, 62-63
  habit tracking, 135, 138, 144-145, 159
  Log Your Thoughts worksheet, 82-83
  mindfulness as an aid to monitoring, 60, 138
  monitoring worksheet, 152
  observation of habits as bringing up feelings, 146-147
  Positive Thoughts, Emotions, and Habits Log, 90
  in Track Your Habits worksheet, 70-71
  visual representations, assistance of, 70, 72
  weekly celebrations sheet, 111
Habits, general, 3, 116, 138, 151
  affirmations and, 58-59
  behaviors, distinguishing from habits, 5, 12
  big problems, breaking into small habits, 21
  box breathing for habit challenges, 130
  case studies in tackling, 4, 138
  celebrations, reinforcing good habits with, 104, 110
  consequences, consciously examining, 105, 112

distractions, removing, 149
goals, aligning habits with, 11, 53, 143
habit loops, 21, 109, 112
in Healthy Habits Brainstorm List, 57
journal prompts on, 59, 80, 97, 117, 139
in One New Prompt activity, 106
"perfect," challenging the idea of, 81
S.M.A.R.T. goals, helping to achieve, 40-41

M

Mindfulness, 15, 50, 93, 133, 149
  box breathing as a mindfulness practice, 130
  brainstorming, mindfulness during, 57
  current habits, mindful awareness of, 60
  difficult emotions, managing with mindfulness techniques, 119
  emotions and actions, staying aware of, 159
  FOCUS Technique for Mindful Awareness, 143
  goals, mindful reflection to reconnect with, 142
  habit change, as a strategy for, 20, 23, 24
  habit loops, mindful awareness of, 112
  in Habits Progress Quiz, 140-141
  how a habit makes you feel, assessing, 146-147
  mindful awareness of habits, increasing, 72
  Mindful Consumption Practice, 66
  Mindful habits, case study in developing, 16
  Mindful Movement for Reflection activity, 148
  mindfulness breaks, scheduling, 85

mindfulness habits, maintaining, 138
Mindfulness Techniques Log, 153
Mindful Visualization of Your
    Future Self, 48
mini-mindfulness breaks as
    check-ins, 76
in Positive Habits Calendar, 67
teeth-brushing, mindful
    engagement in, 102
of thoughts, emotions, and habits, 90
Three Minutes of Mindfulness
    Check-In, 84
Turning Off Autopilot exercise, 47
urge surfing as a mindfulness
    strategy, 116, 135
in Your Environments as Antecedents
    practice, 103
Motivation, 53, 79, 100
  affirmations as motivating, 134
  celebrations as boosting, 111
  journal prompt on, 147
  in Reconnect with Your Goals activity, 142
  social supports, using for, 64, 72
Movement, 61, 96, 148

N

Negative Thoughts, awareness of, 77, 78

P

Positive Thoughts, planning for, 77, 89
Procrastination, 32, 49, 129

R

Reflection, 159
  building awareness through
    reflection, 135
  celebratory reflection, 104, 154-155

mindful reflection, 105, 142, 148
past habits, reflecting on as useful,
    34, 50
in Reconnect with Your Goals
    activity, 142

S

Self-Awareness, 1, 4, 8
  behavior modification and, 19
  mindfulness, building for, 16, 20, 138
  in One New Prompt activity, 106
  self-accountability and, 24
Self Check-Ins, 135
Self-Compassion, 3, 9, 23, 111, 141, 161
Self-Congratulations, 67, 81
Self-Sabotage, 7
  affirmations, countering
    with, 58, 134
  box breathing strategy for, 130
  Common Ways to Self-Sabotage
    assessment, 129
  in Know Your Tendencies
    Quiz, 118-119
  lack of willpower, not indicating, 135
  reflection exercises on, 128, 132-133
Setbacks, 9, 16, 23, 143, 161
Success
  affirmations as encouraging, 134
  celebrating successes, 154-155
  defining success for yourself, 138
  in Habit Progress Quiz, 140-141
  journal prompts on, 37, 139, 147, 150
  Reflect for Success activity, 132-133
  self-sabotaging your success, 129
  smaller habits as the way to, 69
Support Systems, 8, 46, 64

T

U

V

W

Acknowledgments

I am eternally grateful for the many people in my life who've either directly or indirectly supported me during the creation of this book. A special thanks to Bianca Rodriguez for her relentless encouragement, Eun H. Jeong for her superb editing skills, and Jean Brennan for being the best mentor anyone could ask for.

To my biggest sources of inspiration and motivation—Andrew, Thomas, and Sophia—ustedes tres son mi razón de ser.

Lastly, thank you to all the clients I've had the privilege of working with. Being able to support others as a mental health clinician has been one of the greatest honors of my life. Thank you for teaching me empathy, resilience, and what it means to be human.

About the Author

 **Stephanie Sorady Arias, MSW,** is an associate clinical social worker with more than five years of experience in the mental health field. She has worked with a wide variety of folks, such as college students, fellow children of immigrants, people experiencing homelessness, and military veterans. These opportunities have provided Stephanie with diverse perspectives that she uses in her therapeutic practice regularly. Stephanie received her B.A. in social sciences with an emphasis in psychology from the University of Southern California and her master's in social work from Columbia University. She was born and raised in Los Angeles, California, where she currently resides.